Landigal

A Company 1/32 Infantry
10th Mountain Division
Korangal Valley
Kunar Province
Afghanistan
3 August 2006

James F. Christ

Landigal: by James F. Christ

Cover design by Scott Lewis

Edited by Caitlin Taylor

For information address:
1111 North Mission Park Blvd #2031
Chandler, AZ 85224

ISBN 978-0-9788604-1-7

Acknowledgements

There are so many soldiers to thank for the writing of this book that it is hard to know where to start. The path is intricate and obviously a gift from God. ETT 1st Sergeant Don Longfield was interviewed for a different book. He put the author through to his former CO, Lieutenant Colonel Pat Coen, who gave emails for a number of his soldiers, one of whom was Corporal Dustin Hansen. All these men were ETTs. Hansen had one single 10th Mountain email contact—Sergeant Les Garcia of Combat Company 1/32 who served during 2006. (The author never spoke to Les and only shared a few emails with him, asking for interviews with 10th Mountain soldiers.) Garcia was kind enough to say he would send out a few emails, but he was still overseas on a second tour in Afghanistan and had only a few minutes on the internet each week.

Rewind . . . before that, Hansen gave the author another contact. ETT Paul Zuzzio (who served in the Korangal Valley from August to December 2006) was interviewed for an ETT book about the Korangal. During that interview Zuzzio said, "You know, you're writing about ETTs, but the real story is with Attack Company, Tenth Mountain in the Korangal." The author agreed but had no contact information. Zuzzio then supplied the email address for the Attack Company commander, Major Jim McKnight. The author interviewed McKnight but had no idea where to start. Months went by, and the author was stumped, when out of the blue, Specialist Nick Bratland emailed this one single sentence: "I hear you're lookin' for guys who served?" He had received a Facebook message from Les Garcia. He was the only soldier to respond to Garcia's many emails. Bratland fought at Landigal. That is what led to this book. Bratland put the author through to the rest of his company.

A grateful thank you for the interviews from these brave soldiers who served their country so valiantly, gave so much, and very nearly gave everything 3 August 2006 at Landigal:

Chase Gean
Benjamin Bleidorn
Adam Gordon
Jae Barclay
Nick Bratland
Joshua Caracciolo
Robert Duncan II
Khuong Hang
Christopher Quinalty
Neil Yusella

I offer a grateful thank you to these soldiers who also served 3 August 2006 at the KOP, on the QRF, or at Kandigal: (alphabetically) John "Jeb" Brown, Randall Carter, Gary Dales, Daniel Hewerdine, Joshua Lomen, Patrick McClure, James McKnight, Larry North, Tate Preston, John Rush, Blaine Stevens, and Shane Wilkinson.

Other soldiers, some National Guard ETTs, some 1/32 Infantry who deserve credit for assisting the author with interviews, photos, or emails are (alphabetically) Joe Evans, Paul Garcia, Chuck Martin, Sean McQuade, Mike Mulherin, Robert Stanton, Leroy Strickland, Bill Wilkinson, and Paul Zuzzio.

I would like to thank my friends Maurice McSorely, Marty Boetel, Morgan Neville, and Andrew Robles.

I would like to thank Maja Aleksic, Annette and Doyle Madsen, Som Sok, and the staff at CTA Goodman Elementary School—in particular, Anna Pfau, Brooke Sawyer, and Amanda Tietjen—for being so good to my children.

I would like to thank my brother John Joseph Christ, my best friend Jay Templeton, and my father and mother, John Michael Christ and Peggy Ann Christ, for all they have done for me and my sons, Nolan and Trace. No one knows how much you've helped me over this last, trying year, and I am grateful.

And thank you to Jeff Angle and Angela Schlett, without whose help this book would not have been published. Thank you so much!

To my sons Nolan and Trace, I love you; I hope you and your generation appreciate the incredible sacrifice made by so many of our nation's brave sons.

And lastly, because it is the most important, to the Lord God, I love You. Thank You for everything You've done for me.

Introduction

On 3 August 2006, thirteen US soldiers of the 2nd Platoon, A Company, 1/32 10th Mountain Division were given a mission to cordon and search what was arguably the most dangerous village, in the most dangerous valley, in the most dangerous province of war-torn Afghanistan.

Sent out with Afghan National Army soldiers in support, the patrol moved out to accomplish its mission. However, the Afghan soldiers in support of their American counterparts left them, returning to the safety of their base. The Americans were ordered to remain on mission even after radio intercepts warned of an impending attack on the thirteen-man patrol.

The platoon leader in command, knowing their situation was dire and that the enemy was closing in on them, made a decision, which was to him the only option to keep his soldiers, and himself, alive. This is what happened. . . .

(The author wishes to emphasize that opinions are strictly those of the soldiers involved and not of the author. They are simply statements either quoted or paraphrased from the individuals being interviewed.)

Foreword

"If you want the God's-honest truth, no one will admit it, but the biggest issue facing these men, including myself, is to deal with knowing how much we could have accomplished if we'd had the leadership to do it. Most of these guys had dreams of changing the world, and with the men we had, we know we could have. We could have done a lot over there, but we were hamstrung. And not just killing the bad guys but really helping the people over there, and we weren't able to.

"The frustration gnaws at a lot of us, and it's been a secret we've kept for years; you watch the news and know most people don't want to hear what's really going on over there . . . knowing others will get to read it makes it worth bringing back all the God-awful memories.

"As far as we're concerned, no one could understand what it was like over there. All we had were each other to talk to, and since we've all gone our separate ways, and haven't had anyone to share with, and a lot of us didn't want to talk to each other because of the lurking feelings. And when we talk to civilians, we tend to hold back because we don't want to get the 'crazy vet' label that haunted the guys from Vietnam. People tend to seem patronizing, which frustrates us even more, so we just learned to shut up. As a historian it bothered me to think our story would never become a part of the written record."

This is from a series of text messages sent to the author by Adam Gordon. Keep in mind; this was not in reference to this Landigal book but the much broader time of his brothers in the Korangal Valley from May 2006 to May 2007. Nor did Gordon have any idea when he sent the texts that the author was going to find them so honest and powerful that he would use them as a foreword for this book.

Acronyms

AAR	After Action Report
ACM	Anti-Coalition Militia
ACU	Army Combat Uniform
ANA	Afghan National Army
AO	Area of Operation
BC	Battalion Commander
BDE	Brigade
BDU	Battle Dress Uniform
BN	Battalion
CAS	Close Air Support
CLS	Combat Life Saver
CCP	Casualty Collection Point
CO	Commanding Officer
CP	Command Post
CPT	Captain
CSM	Command Sergeant Major
DCU	Desert Combat Uniform
ETT	Embedded Tactical Trainer
FNG	Fucking New Guy
FO	Forward Observer
FSO	Fire Support Officer
FSNCOIC	Fire Support Non-Commissioned Officer
GCP	Ground Commanders Pointer
HA	Humanitarian Assistance
HLZ	Helicopter Landing Zone
HMMWV	High Mobile Multi Wheeled Vehicle
HQ	Headquarters
HVT	High Value Target
IED	Improvised Explosive Device
JTAC	Joint Tactical Aircraft Controller
KOP	Korangal Outpost
LT	Lieutenant
LTC	Lieutenant Colonel
LZ	Landing Zone
MBITR	Multiband Inter/Intra Team Radio
MOLLE	Mobular Lightweight Load-carrying Equipment

MRE	Meal Ready to Eat
NCO	Non-Commissioned Officer
NCOIC	Non-Commissioned Officer In Charge
OIC	Officer In Charge
OP	Outpost
OPFOR	Opposing Force
PL	Platoon Leader
QRF	Quick Reaction Force
R&R	Rest and Recuperation
RIP	Relief In Place
RPG	Rocket-Propelled Grenade
1SG	First Sergeant
SITREP	Situation Report
SF	Special Forces
SFC	Sergeant First Class
SGT	Sergeant
SOP	Standard Operating Procedure
SPC	Specialist
SSG	Staff Sergeant
THT	Tactical Humint (Human Intelligence) Team
TIC	Troops In Contact
TFP	Task Force Phoenix
TOC	Tactical Operations Center
TRP	Target Reference Point

Weapons (Chart by Paul Zuzzio)

Rifle	Caliber	MAX Effective Range
US M4 Carbine	5.56x45mm	500m
ANA/ACM AK-47	7.62x39mm	400m
Light Machinegun		
US M249 SAW	5.56x45mm	1000m
ANA/ACM RPK	7.62x39mm	1000m
Medium Machinegun		
US M240B	7.62x51mm	800m
ANA/ACM PKM	7.62x54mm	1500m
Heavy Machinegun		
US M2HB	.50cal/12.7x99mm	1800m
ANA/ACM DshK	12.7x108mm	2000m
Grenade Launchers		
US M203	40x46mm	400m
US Mk-19	40x53mm	1500m
ANA/ACM RPG-7	85mm	920m

Heavy Weapons	Caliber/Size	MAX Effective
US 60mm Mortar	60mm/3-4lb	3400m
US 120mm Mortar	120mm/20lb	7240m
US 155mm M198	155mm/103lb	30,000m
ANA/ACM SPG-9	73mm/Approx 3lb	6500m
ANA/ACM mortar	82mm/3lb	4100m
ANA/ACM	107mm Rocket	8050m

Aircraft	Crew	Load
US A-10 "Warthog"	1-2	1 30mm Gatling Cannon

(Up to 11 hardpoints and 16,000 lbs of rockets or bombs.)

Aircraft	Crew	Load
US AH-64 "Apache"	2	1 30mm Chain Gun

(Up to 4 hard points and up to 70 2.75in rockets.)

US UH-60 "Blackhawk"	4	Up to 14 troops or 6 stretchers

(2 Gun Mounts with up to 7.62 miniguns or M2 .50 cal.)

Landigal

James F. Christ

"O Lord, how many are my adversaries!
Many rise up against me!"

Psalm 3:1

"Soldiers and officers alike should read these notes and seek to apply their lessons. We *must* cash in on the experience which these and other brave men have paid for in blood."

General George C. Marshall

It is the author's hope that future officers and enlisted personnel of the US Military will benefit from these books, but also that the wounded, injured, traumatized, and haunted veterans of these actions will find solace and healing in the opportunity to read about the events in which they became physical and emotional casualties.

"We knew the south was bad. We knew it was going to be a shit-hole, and we were about to step into it, but we had no concept of how bad it was going to be. The freakin' ANA knew because they decided not to come with us. You always get the brief, 'This is going to be a dangerous mission.' This was the Korangal Valley; everyplace is dangerous. But nobody knew how well armed and organized they were. That was the big surprise, how organized they were. They weren't just rock farmers with AK-forty-sevens. Obviously these guys understood military strategy, or they wouldn't have been able to pull off a multi-point fuckin' ambush on us in the middle of a freakin' valley." Corporal Robert Duncan III, 2nd Platoon, A Company, 1st Battalion, 32nd Infantry, 3rd Brigade Combat Team, 10th Mountain Division.

The KOP
0030; 3 August 2006

"Hmmm," thought Sergeant Adam Gordon (age 22) of Heath, Ohio. "What's this about?" Gordon was a six-foot-six-inch, 190-pound Forward Observer (FO) waiting in full battle rattle to go out on patrol with a squad of soldiers from the 2nd Platoon, A Company, 1st Battalion, 32nd Infantry, 10th Mountain Division.

Gordon watched their company commander, Captain James McKnight (age 29) of upstate New York, walk up to the patrol. Everyone turned to hear what their CO had to say. It was rare for him to come over to a patrol just before it was preparing to head out. He always spoke to whoever was leading the patrol, but seldom to the soldiers on the patrol. McKnight stopped in front of his men and told them he wanted to lead them in a prayer before they moved out. He asked everyone to gather closer together and kneel.

PFC Christopher "Q" Quinalty (age 22) of Tyler, Texas, listened intently as his CO bent his head in supplication. Quinalty was grateful for a prayer. Quinalty's personal opinion was that all people, especially soldiers in a combat zone, should stay right with the Lord, as God was the only one that was going to be looking out for them.

1

"God, protect us on our journey," said McKnight, "and bring us back safely."

While Quinalty's thoughts were appreciative, Gordon's thoughts were, "Why?" McKnight had never held a prayer service before a patrol headed out. He held Bible studies, but he had never come down and said a prayer with a unit before. Why was he having one now? Everyone knew the village where they were going was a bad place. Since American/coalition forces had been in the valley, they had been fired on every single time they went in the vicinity of it. Now less than a platoon was preparing to head out, and their CO thought it important enough to come down and personally lead them in prayer. Gordon was creeped out. It seemed to him like a eulogy.

McKnight finished and wished his soldiers well. He returned to the TOC leaving the group standing, looking around at each other.

All Quinalty knew of the mission was what his squad leader had told him: "You need to get your shit ready to head out." That had been an hour ago. Then, through intent listening, he had learned they were going to a village with some ANA. They were never told more than they needed to know. Quinalty knew it was best that way.

CPL Robert Duncan II (Age 22) of Brooklyn, Iowa, was one of the soldiers standing beside Gordon and Quinalty. Duncan was a six-foot-one-inch, 210-pound M-240B gunner. He had been 220 pounds, but two weeks of humping the unforgiving mountains of the Korangal Valley had already made him shed ten pounds. Duncan knew the operation his squad was about to undertake would be two days, and possibly three, so he decided to quickly move over to the Tactical Operations Center (TOC) to call his wife Jaqui. Her birthday was 5 August, two days away. He wanted to call her just in case the mission dragged on and they got back late. Duncan didn't want his wife to think he'd forgotten her birthday.

Duncan made his way over to the TOC where the new SIPR (Secure Internet Protocol Routing) phone was hooked up to the computer. Until recently they had been able to call home only once a month, but with the new phone, they could call home twice a week. Only, when Duncan entered the TOC, there were already five guys ahead of him.

"Fuck," he muttered to himself, realizing he wouldn't have time. It was now 0050, and his patrol was leaving at 0100. Duncan was just turning to leave when SFC John Rush (age 28) of Philadelphia, Pennsylvania, stopped him.

"You're going to Landigal, right?"

"Yeah."

"You need to call your wife."

"Oh," said Duncan, "okay." It was the way Rush said it that took Duncan aback. Rush told the five soldiers waiting to let Duncan go ahead. It struck Duncan as he reached for the phone: He was going on a very dangerous patrol.

Duncan was in arguably the most dangerous area of the planet—the Korangal Valley, Afghanistan. Duncan was a team leader in the 2nd Squad, 2nd Platoon. Their squad was tasked with patrolling to the village of Landigal where they would conduct a cordon and search with a squad of Afghan National Army (ANA) soldiers. The Americans would cordon the area and provide over-watch from the ridgeline—hopefully unseen by the civilians—while the ANA with their American Embedded Tactical Trainer (ETT) searched the village. This was an attempt at letting the ANA assert itself in the valley and show the Afghans in the Korangal that their own country's army was in control. The patrol was also tasked with making an assessment of Landigal while meeting the village elders. It was hoped that they might establish relations that might lead to future friendships. At least, that was how the patrol was written up on paper.

Since Attack Company's arrival in the last days of May, the situation in the Korangal had become increasingly violent. The Americans were still new to the valley and trying to learn and understand the political and tribal infrastructure of the powers-that-be in the Korangal. It was far more complex than they could have imagined. First, the entire area was like a series of armed camps and had been for hundreds of years. Army after

3

army had bled themselves to death and been unable to tame the Korangal.

In August of 2006, among the many factions vying for power in the valley, at the top of the power hierarchy sat the Korangali Timber Barons. The Korangal and its surrounding valleys were heavily forested, or had been before they had been cleared of timber. Only, the new Afghan National Government was trying to declare itself in the region and told the Timber Barons they could only sell their timber to the government— for a set price, and for a specified amount. This was because One, the government was trying to protect the last heavily forested, non-desert region in their country; and, two, the Timber Barons were selling their timber to Pakistan at a marked-up rate, and it was then being resold back to Afghanistan at an even higher price.

The Timber Barons were angry at being regulated and losing their primary source of income. They became anti-outsider, uncooperative, and covertly aggressive toward anyone in support of or representing the new government.

Then there were the two main tribes in the Korangal Valley: The Korangalis and Safis. Both practiced the Wahabbis sect of Islam usually identified with Saudi Arabia and Osama Bin Laden. The Korangalis were originally a tribe from Nuristan. However, a century before, there had been a war, and the Nuristanis had won. The Korangalis lost and were forced out of Nuristan. They fled eastward and moved into the valleys of what is now the Korangal. They quickly grew in strength and now inhabited the southern region of the Korangal. The Korangalis spoke their own language but also spoke Pashto because they were surrounded by Safis, who spoke Pashto.

The tribe to the north was the Safis. They were just as fiercely independent as the Korangalis. Their region of influence was mainly along the Pesch River Valley but also extended into the northern reaches of the Korangal.

When the United States looked for a location to set up an outpost in the Korangal Valley, the powers-that-be picked the only piece of flat ground in the entire valley—an area called "The Lumber Yard." Now that area was called "the KOP" for the Korangal Outpost and was the battle space HQs for Attack Company of the 1st Battalion, 32nd Infantry, 10th Mountain Division.

Unbeknownst to the Americans when they first selected the spot, the Lumber Yard was directly between the two tribes. Once discovered, that was seen as both good and bad—good because the US/coalition forces were neutral, and bad because the two tribes were almost constantly fighting. To the US soldiers, the tribes resembled the Hatfields and the McCoys in the way they would constantly make retaliatory blood vengeance attacks on one another.

Of lesser power and influence were the different village elders, who of course were basically sub-commanders within the two tribes (there are six major sub-tribes within the Korangali tribe), but each with a certain degree of autonomy where they directed the goings-on in their particular area of the valley. Aside from the fact that the people in the valley considered themselves Korangalis or Safis first, not Afghans, and resented the Afghan National Government's presence, these communities were extremely territorial. Although very eager to make money, they were equally as opposed to outsiders being in their area and fiercely oppositional to anyone telling them what to do.

Then there were the jihadists from the many reaches of the Muslim world—a majority of which hailed from Pakistan—who looked upon the Korangal as a Muslim "Remember the Alamo" type of battle cry. Fighters training in Pakistan surged to the Korangal over most other areas of Afghanistan as it was almost sacred ground—the nerve center of the ACM—and as al-Qaeda and ACM leadership recognized the Korangal as the most likely spot for a strategic victory against the United States and its coalition allies. They believed this because of the remoteness of its location, the miniscule size of the US forces in the Korangal itself, the unforgiving terrain, and the history of the independent fighters that inhabited the valley. The population was ripe for insurgent activity.

On top of that, the mountains were formidable, and the United States had a single battalion holding the Pesch Valley, the Waygol Valley, the Shiriak Valley, and the Korangal. To give an example of how few those numbers were and, at the same time, to show the formidable fighting ability of the Korangalis and the Safis, in the 1980s, the Soviet Union entered the Korangal Valley with a considerably larger force, the army of one of the world's two superpowers. When the Soviets finally decided to pull out of Afghanistan, a force larger than that the Americans were sending was all that remained to limp out. The rest of the Soviet troops were buried in the Korangal or evacuated by convoy to hospitals or cemeteries.[i]

In August 2006, to take on that formidable valley with years of history defeating army after army, the United States had a grand total of 110 men—Alpha Company, more commonly referred to by its soldiers as "Attack" Company. And their numbers were up from the single Platoon of C Company, 1st Battalion, 32nd Infantry under Lieutenant Sean McQuade that held the valley in May 2006. McQuade had inherited the valley from the Marines, who pulled their battalion out when McQuade's soldiers RIP-ed in.

Now, over two months later, attempting to build alliances and friendship within the valley proved to be an increasingly difficult endeavor. The local population lived in fear of almost everyone in the valley except the Americans. This was mainly because the Americans did not nail the decapitated head of a local to a village door to make an example of someone suspected of dealing with the opposition—something the ACM has no problem doing, was very good at, and did to great effect.[ii]

Then there was the end of May Shura. That was when the Attack Company CO held his first meeting with the Korangal elders. In early May when McQuade came in, for the purposes of self-preservation, knowing he had only forty men in the valley, the young lieutenant was extremely diplomatic. McQuade would spend entire days meeting with the many village elders at their homes, sipping Chai tea and eating lunch and dinner with them. With no experience at diplomacy and only his civilian experience in law enforcement to draw on,

McQuade would sit down with men he knew were bad—who he knew were lying to him—and attempt to build relationships that he hoped would lead to future friendships and possible alliances. Whether or not McQuade could have done that will never be known. His platoon RIP-ed out at the end of July to rejoin Combat Company on the Pesch while Attack Company took over in the Korangal.[iii]

Before McQuade left, Alpha Company came in with its headquarters element and one single platoon (its other two infantry platoons were deployed elsewhere). The Alpha Company and Bravo Company commanders held a Shura with all the village elders in the valley.[iv] After that night, the situation in the valley seemed to change. In May, when McQuade's C Company platoon was alone at the KOP, they had numerous TICs but no casualties. Since that end of May Shura, the number of TICs went through the roof starting with a multi-point attack on the KOP on 3 June. Unexplainably, when patrols were ambushed, they were almost always the A Company platoon. It became a running joke between McQuade and the A Company platoon leader (LT Tate Preston) because McQuade's C Company platoon was always coming to bail them out as a Quick Reaction Force (QRF).

Coincidence? Possibly. But several soldiers felt things changed violently because of breaches in etiquette toward the valley elders.[v] The Korangalis and Safis both lived the Pashtunwali Code, a way of life based on nine principles: Justice, Bravery, Loyalty, Righteousness, Trust in Allah, Dignity, Hospitality, Chivalry, and Vengeance. Disrespect toward an elder could cause a state of "Badal" or blood vengeance, which would have to be paid for in blood whether vengeance was made the following day or a thousand years later. In Afghan and Korangali culture, it simply could not go unpunished.

Unfortunately, one's estranged enemies can become friends, and alliances and friendships were forged among the timber barons, the many village elders, and the al-Qaeda and ACM. The result was that the Korangal Valley was an extremely dangerous place for a United States soldier to be—if not the *most* dangerous place in the world.

Surprisingly, a great many Americans in the United States knew nothing of the war their soldiers were fighting. Aside from a handful that knew the truth, most believed the enemy to be Muslim hillbillies with AK-47s firing wildly at US soldiers. Unfortunately, that was simply not the case. The enemy was well trained, extremely well armed, and directed by experienced leadership. On top of that, they had great numbers and believed fanatically in their cause. It was this enemy against whom Duncan and the rest of the 2nd Squad were preparing to move out.

Duncan knew he didn't have much time and spoke quickly to his wife. He asked how their newborn baby was. Duncan had just returned from emergency leave. Two weeks before, he had been allowed to return to Iowa because of complications with his son's birth. Robert Duncan III had to undergo emergency open-heart surgery immediately after he was born. It had taken two days just for Duncan to get home. Then, two days after the operation, with his wife still in the hospital and his son hanging on to life in the neo-natal ICU, Duncan was ordered to return to Afghanistan. He arrived back at the KOP one week later. Now he was preparing to head out on a cordon search of a village named Landigal.

"I love you," said Duncan to his wife after he'd used up his minutes. He hung up and thanked Rush, who was himself waiting to get on the phone to call his own wife. Rush was in the 1st Platoon, and his unit was preparing to move out to the north to a village called Kandigal. They would leave at 0200, an hour after Duncan's patrol.

Duncan moved back to his unit. Twelve men were standing or sitting, waiting for their Afghan National Army (ANA) counterparts to arrive. It was Standard Operating Procedure (SOP) that US or coalition troops were not supposed to move unless they were supporting ANA troops.

It was now 0100, and Duncan wanted to light up a cigarette but he couldn't. He had to wait for first light. Duncan sat down, glancing at his watch from time to time. The minutes ticked by.

Soon 0115 came and went, and still there was no sign of the ANA troops they were to accompany. There were also no orders to move out. Duncan wasn't surprised. He lay back against the Hesco revetment and tried to doze. Someone would wake him when the time came.

0130; ETT TOC; near the LZ: Lieutenant Daniel Hewerdine (age 36) of Saint Louis, Missouri, was a Ready Reservist who'd been called up to active duty. He was the senior Embedded Tactical Trainer (ETT) working with the ANA troops in the Korangal Outpost. Hewerdine was supposed to have several other National Guard ETTs working with him, but there was a manpower shortage all over Afghanistan, and US forces were stretched to the bone. Because of that, Hewerdine had only one other ETT. They were supposed to have a total of four. Trying to fill the slots, Task Force Phoenix had attempted to bolster their ranks by adding two Security Forces (SECFOR) personnel from the Oklahoma National Guard. They weren't ETTs, but they were bodies, and they would have to do.

Hewerdine was trying to juggle the needs of the ANA troops he oversaw, the missions with which the 10th Mountain company commander was asking for cooperation, and the responsibilities of the ANA commander he mentored. Right now he was faced with dual multi-day missions to the north and south, and at the same time he had to keep enough forces to defend the KOP.

The Attack Company commander was sending two patrols out: a larger three-day patrol to Kandigal in the north (to link with an incoming platoon) and a smaller two-day patrol to Landigal in the south. And he was sending them at the same time. That presented a problem. Hewerdine didn't understand why the mission to the south couldn't wait, but his job was not to question why, but instead to try to get the ANA commander to cooperate with the Attack Company commander.

Hewerdine's problem was this: There were only 55 ANA troops in the entire Korangal Outpost. He had a request for ten ANA to move to the north and ten ANA to head out with the patrol moving south. That alone wasn't an insurmountable problem because they had 55 troops from whom to select. Hewerdine's problem was that the ANA commander had a completely different mindset from that of the Attack Company commander.

The ANA commander did not like to send out missions and told Hewerdine so—his reason being that he didn't see them as important or useful. For one thing, he didn't believe the locals could be won over. They were not like other Afghans. The ANA commander explained to Hewerdine his one concern: He had orders not to let his base be overrun. That would be an intolerable embarrassment to the new government. The ANA commander had expressed this to Hewerdine on more than one occasion. Faced with dual missions where the American commander wanted him to send out one third of his force, he was less than cooperative.

The ANA commander told Hewerdine over and over that the 10th Mountain commander sent out too many missions. His Afghan soldiers were always rotating in and out on multi-day patrols and were perennially tired. He also told Hewerdine he thought the American troops were even more exhausted. Their commander pushed them too hard. The ANA commander said his men who had just come back from missions needed rest. If he was sending out two more patrols, the men going out combined with the exhausted men coming in left him very few men with whom to operate their base and man their perimeter.

Regardless of whether or not Hewerdine agreed with him, Attack Company had two patrols moving out and was requesting ANA troops to accompany them. Hewerdine had no choice but to press the ANA commander to fill both missions.

From the start, the ANA commander was opposed to the patrol heading to the south. Every time they went south, they had contact. He stalled on getting troops for that mission. He did, however, come up with ten ANA soldiers to move to the north. Whether it was because sending men to the north was not as dangerous as sending a patrol to Landigal or because the American contingent moving north was larger in size remained to be seen, but at least Hewerdine was able to muster an RPG team, a PKM team, an RPK team, and a team of infantry to accompany the 1st Platoon.

Although the patrol should be heading out with an ETT, Hewerdine was the only ETT at the KOP. His fellow ETT, Staff Sergeant (SSG) Chuck Martin (age 46) of Darington, Washington, was back at Kabul clearing FOO and bringing in Hewerdine's replacement, SSG Paul Zuzzio (age 34) of Lawrenceville, New Jersey, so he couldn't go. But as the ETT commander, Hewerdine couldn't leave on a three-day mission. His duty was to mentor the ANA commander and monitor their base defenses, among his other logistical and administrative duties.

That left the two SECFOR soldiers from whom to choose. Hewerdine decided to send Sergeant Dennis McClain (age 22) of Oklahoma with the ANA patrol heading north. Hewerdine gave him the basic brief, and McClain headed to the LZ where the ANA were assembling near the 10th Mountain troops to start their mission.

0150; Attack Main TOC: Rush was in the Attack Main TOC. Like Duncan, he had long since finished his phone call to his wife and was preparing to head out on a separate mission. Rush and his platoon leader (PL), Lieutenant Tate Preston (age 26) of Chathem, New Jersey, were about to head out to the north. Preston was the PL for the 1st Platoon. Rush was the platoon sergeant. Their platoon was tasked with a dual mission. Attack Main had intel on a High Value Target (HVT) residing in the village of Kandigal. They were to find and arrest the HVT for removal to Asadabad. They were also to secure the Kandigal area for their 3rd Platoon's entry into the valley.

Until the arrival of the 2nd Platoon, up to now Attack Company had only one of its three platoons. (For the last two months it had been bolstered by McQuade's Combat Company platoon, which had been there prior to A Company's arrival, but McQuade's platoon had just recently been removed to the Pesch to rejoin the rest of Combat Company less than a week ago.) With the arrival of the 3rd Platoon, Attack Company

11

would finally have all three of its infantry platoons together again after several months of independent operations.

With final preparations complete, Preston and Rush moved out of the TOC and over to their assembly area. It was almost 0200. They were leaving under the cover of darkness because whenever they headed anywhere by day, there seemed to be a lot more contact with the enemy. By leaving at nightfall they hoped to keep the ACM from being forewarned, as the enemy did not seem to have night vision.

0200; Hescos near the KOP LZ: Duncan, Gordon, and Quinalty sat waiting. The 2nd squad, 2nd Platoon had originally been told they would leave at 0100. Only, like most things in the Army, orders inexplicably changed. They had been waiting in the darkness near the LZ until their own PL told them to move over to the Hescos to await the ANA. Now it was 0200 and they were still there. Duncan and Gordon watched the 1st Platoon patrol move out and head down the road to the north. Soon the tread of their marching feet could no longer be heard as they moved away into the night. Duncan drifted back to sleep aware that they'd wake him when he needed to know what was going on.

ETT TOC: Hewerdine received a call from Attack Main wondering when the ANA squad would be ready to head south to Landigal. Hewerdine had no time frame to give. The ANA commander was still resistant to the idea. He wasn't refusing outright; he was simply stalling and had not yet assembled any soldiers for the patrol. Hewerdine could only advise the ANA commander; he couldn't order him to do anything. The ANA officer told him he would get the troops ready. When that would be, Hewerdine didn't know.

Hewerdine called Attack Main and told McKnight what the ANA commander said. Then Hewerdine turned to his remaining SECFOR soldier, Specialist Nate Kraus (age 19) of Oklahoma. Kraus was the ETT stand-in who would be moving out with the ANA to Landigal. Hewerdine told Kraus to be ready to move when the ANA assembled.

0215; LT Preston's Platoon; Kuz Obinaw: The 1st Platoon was making good time. They had just passed Kuz Obinaw and were moving along the bumpy, pockmarked Korangal Road. They were only fifteen minutes outside the KOP, but already they were covered in the moon-dust-like powder that was ubiquitous of the Korangal. Since they were moving at night, it was much cooler, and the oppressive heat of daytime wasn't sapping their strength. Each American soldier was weighed down with almost eighty pounds of equipment and body armor. The ANA soldiers in the contingent were significantly less burdened. They had maybe 25 pounds of weapons, supplies, and equipment. They seemed to be unaware of the difference in weight loads because they were notorious for complaining to their ETT and SECFOR mentors that the Americans were slow.

There were 34 personnel on the patrol made up of twenty American soldiers, ten ANA, their ETT stand-in, a THT soldier, and two Afghan interpreters. The Americans wore night vision, and the patrol moved relatively unseen to the north on schedule. They left Kuz Obinaw behind and continued toward Kandigal. The next major village they would pass would be Camersa Banda to the east, maybe an hour and a half farther down the road.

0300; ETT TOC; near the LZ: Hewerdine still sat waiting for word about the Landigal patrol. He had called the ANA commander's hooch several times that night asking for an arrival time on the ANA troops. The ANA commander said he would assemble them, but it had been three hours, and there were still no troops available. Hewerdine called over to the Attack Main TOC and gave McKnight the latest. The ANA were on the way; he just didn't know when.

Attack Main TOC: McKnight was in the TOC with his Executive Officer (XO) LT Gary Dales (age 27) of Manning, Iowa. The two usually slept on cots right outside the TOC, but tonight there was no sleep. They were still waiting on the ANA for the 2nd Platoon and monitoring the 1st Platoon's movement down to Kandigal.

McKnight was a five-foot-five-inch, 160-pound graduate of Washington & Lee University in Lexington, Virginia, who did his ROTC at the Virginia Military Institute. McKnight had just recently returned to the KOP after convalescing from injuries sustained when he fell off a cliff while on patrol over a month before. He had broken several bones, and it was a miracle he had even survived at all. McKnight had been laid up in Asadabad for a month.

McKnight had wanted to get back to his command so badly that he approached the doctor to sign his release, but was given one stipulation: "No dismounted patrolling for sixty days." McKnight had agreed, and on 30 July he flew back out. It was now five days later, and he and his lieutenants had planned a mission to Landigal.

McKnight had been given the broad mission of separating the local population from the enemy in the Korangal Valley— something he knew would be extremely difficult with the manpower he had.

McKnight had asked his battalion commander for additional support, but there was none. In all of Afghanistan there was only one single US brigade and one single aviation brigade to support it. All US resources were tied up in Iraq. McKnight's BC had told him, "You got to figure out how to do what you can with what you got."

The BC explained that their brigade's mission was essentially an economy of force. They were holding in Afghanistan so that the weight of the US armed forces might be able to win the war in Iraq. Whether or not that was going to work remained to be seen, but it stressed US forces in Afghanistan to the limit, especially in the Korangal. Even with that explanation, however, the BC was very aggressive and asked all of his company commanders to take the fight to the enemy at all times—especially in the Korangal.

The Korangal Valley was one of the primary locations where the enemy recruited the local population to fight against the coalition. The ACM had great success influencing and

14

recruiting from that particular piece of population, and they used this population to conduct attacks, mostly in the Korangal, but also along the Pesch and in other areas of Afghanistan, particularly, but not limited to, Kunar Province.

With Attack Main setting up in the KOP after Operation Mountain Lion, it was basically taking up camp in the enemy's backyard, where the insurgents normally felt safe to hand out money, cache supplies, and rest. McKnight felt that had really set them off balance, at first, and greatly angered them.

The intent of Attack Main, as directed from battalion, was to find and destroy the enemy and at the same time befriend the local population. However, those tasks couldn't be done until they defeated the insurgents that were operating within the Korangal because, unfortunately, the enemy would watch from the mountains. The insurgents would see the ANA and US forces cordon and search a village; they would carefully observe and see just who was speaking to the Americans. Then, as soon as the US forces and their ANA allies left, the insurgents would come in behind them and intimidate the people of the village. They would threaten to kill anyone who cooperated with the Americans. After the first few murders, it had been very difficult to get any cooperation out of the valley.

Of all the places in the valley, the enemy had several known safe havens. Arguably the worst was the village of Landigal. McKnight wanted to move on the village, find any weapons caches that might be there, and deny them to the enemy. He hoped to show the villagers that the ANA controlled the valley and were getting stronger while the insurgents were getting weaker. He wanted to dismantle their recruiting base and at the same time begin rapport that could lead to friendships and alliances.

McKnight had planned this particular mission with his two platoon lieutenants. His company was not fully intact as the 3rd Platoon had been committed elsewhere, but it was finally on the way and would cross the Pesch within 24 hours. That was one reason why Preston's 1st Platoon was going down to the river.

15

In the meantime, McKnight didn't want to sit idly and wait for his company to reach full strength. He wanted to take the fight to the enemy and deny them their strongholds.

"Look," said McKnight to his 2nd Platoon leader. "Go cordon search the village like we normally do, and then go set up a good ambush position somewhere in between Landigal and Donga." Donga was the village between the KOP and Landigal. The enemy was funneling money and weapons into the valley and hiding them in villages like Landigal. They would then pay the local Korangalis to attack the Americans at the KOP. When the money was spent and the ammunition was expended, the locals would melt back into the countryside or return to their villages. Then the ACM would return to Pakistan for more money and more ammunition.

The mission McKnight and his lieutenants designed was to get to Landigal and take the enemy's safe haven from them. They would find their stores of weapons and supplies and try to stop their trafficking. Then, as it would seem to the enemy, the 2nd Platoon patrol would head back to the north in the direction of the KOP. It would then stop, set up an ambush, and try to surprise the insurgents they all knew were operating out of Landigal.

McKnight tailored the force to be thirteen Americans because he knew they would have ANA, and the force would number some 25 men. They were not supposed to be a full platoon on the move because they were supposed to hide. Experience had shown when they sent out a large force, the enemy would simply melt into the countryside. Since they wanted to find and destroy the enemy, they hoped to lure them out with a smaller unit and ambush them for a change. It was an attempt at using the enemy's own guerrilla tactics against them.

McKnight wanted the patrol to leave during the night, but even if it didn't, that was not an insurmountable problem. He often sent patrols out during the day. Sometimes they were seen; sometimes they were not. They were trying to lure the enemy to them. A large force wouldn't be able to do that.

16

0415; LT Preston's Platoon; West of Camersa

Banda: The 1st Platoon was still making good time. Even though it was August and oppressively hot by day, it was cool in the darkness of early morning. Dawn was not far off, but the patrol hoped to be to Kandigal within two hours before the heat sapped their strength.

Rush marched along with his troops and noted there had been no ICOM traffic. Attack Main had a US Prophet Element that monitored the enemy radio frequencies with an Afghan interpreter. Anytime the enemy passed messages, they intercepted what was being said and relayed it to Attack Main, who would then send it out to its different patrols moving in the valley. Since they never knew exactly which element was picking up ICOM, Attack Main sent the message to all its patrols. So far, the radio net was quiet. That was good. It meant the enemy probably did not have eyes on them. That was one of the benefits of moving at night. Every time they moved by day, there was instantly enemy radio traffic pinpointing how many men were moving and in what direction.

The KOP; Hescos near the LZ: Specialist Nick

"Scrappy" Bratland (age 20) of Groton, South Dakota, was sitting with Duncan, Gordon, Quinalty, and the others waiting for orders to move out to Landigal. Bratland was the PL's Radio Telephone Operator (RTO), so he wasn't in a squad but attached to the PL's HQ element with the medic and their Forward Observer (FO). Like Duncan, Bratland was waiting for orders. Word had been passed to them from their platoon leader that the ANA still weren't ready.

Bratland had gotten the nickname Scrappy because of his size and personality. Whereas Duncan was big, Bratland was much smaller, only five feet seven inches and 145 pounds. Where Duncan was easygoing and good-humored, Bratland often had to defend himself, usually verbally, and sometimes from a quarrel he started. Bratland had recently returned to Attack Company after having been wounded by an RPG blast during an ambush in Khogiyani. He had taken shrapnel in the arm and been evacuated over a month ago. Now, he was fully

17

recovered and back with his unit. From what he'd been told, any minute they would be heading out.

0445; LT Preston's Platoon; Tur Kalay: Preston, Rush, and the other soldiers of the 1st Platoon passed Tur Kalay and headed for Kandigal. Because of the mountains, it was still dark, but slivers of light could be seen in the eastern skies. There was still no ICOM, so hopefully the enemy wasn't aware they were moving. They had passed a number of villages throughout the night, so it was possible the enemy knew of a troop movement, but so far there was no radio traffic. If they did know soldiers were on the move, they hadn't reported it yet—probably because they didn't know how many were moving or in what direction the troops were moving.

0500; the KOP LZ: Sergeant Chase Gean (age 25) of Protection, Kansas, sat beside his buddy Sergeant Benjamin "Ben" Bleidorn (age 25) of Madison, Wisconsin. It was Gean's squad that was going out on patrol to Landigal. The two were the primary NCO leadership of the patrol. Both men were squad leaders, but Gean was the squad leader for the 2nd Squad. Bleidorn was going along only because one of Gean's sergeants was on leave, and they needed someone with experience. Bleidorn had volunteered to go as a team leader, and now they sat waiting for orders to head to Landigal.

Bleidorn had expected to leave at 0100. That didn't happen, and he had fallen asleep waiting with the others near the LZ figuring someone would rouse him. Now it was almost dawn, and he was surprised to stir on his own.

"Why haven't we left yet? Why didn't anyone wake me?"

"It got changed," said Gean, who had seen no reason to wake his friend.

"That's stupid!"

Bleidorn looked south down the valley toward Landigal and knew their cover was blown. He could see light in the eastern skies. Soon it would be dawn. Moving in the light of day was like announcing to the enemy with a bullhorn where they were headed and with exactly how many men. And of all

18

places, they were near the LZ. There was no more visible spot in the KOP than the LZ if anyone was watching them from the mountains.

Gean was angry. By now everyone knew the ANA weren't ready, but Gean didn't understand why they were still waiting to leave at any moment. Why couldn't they postpone the operation and leave after nightfall? They had been up all night and were tired. They could rest. Now they would leave at midday, when everyone in the valley, especially the "goat herders" up on the surrounding ridges, could see them leave. The Afghan civilians appeared to be normal villagers up in the mountains, watching their goats—and they probably were—but the one thing they did have was a radio. Everyone suspected the enemy would know exactly how many soldiers were on the patrol the moment they left the KOP.

It was almost dawn now, and everyone was tired from having been up all night sitting with their backs up against the Hescos or lying on their packs. Gean was only a sergeant and had to follow orders, but he didn't understand why moving to Landigal, the worst area in the worst valley, was so important that it necessitated leaving by day. Regardless of the ANA's not showing up, he was convinced their CO was the reason for their daytime departure.

"When do we ever leave during the day?" he asked Bleidorn. "Now that McKnight's back, we leave in the day. The whole valley's going to know how many of us there are and where we're heading. Captain Brown never had us leaving during the day."

Gean had been upset since he'd learned three days ago they were losing CPT John "Jeb" Brown (age 29) of Atlanta, Texas.[vi] Brown had been sent out as a replacement when McKnight had fallen off a cliff. McKnight had been MEDEVAC-ed out, and Brown had flown in to assume command of Attack Company.

Interestingly enough, it was rumored that A Company was originally supposed to have been under Brown's command, but he had been passed over by the BC for McKnight. Brown had been in command for all of three weeks when McKnight returned on 30 July, and now Brown was preparing to head back. At that very moment, Brown was up near the O-P-2 60mm mortar biding his time until a re-supply convoy arrived on 6 August to take him back to Asadabad.

Bleidorn held the same opinion as Gean, but he was less vocal about it. He had flown in on the same helicopter as McKnight four days ago after having returned from R&R. He figured McKnight was looking for a fight, and that was why they were leaving during the day.

"Why couldn't we keep Captain Brown?" said Gean aloud. Bleidorn knew his friend was venting. Most everyone had liked Brown and thought him a fine and able commander. Only a rare few seemed to like McKnight, and most of them were in his HQ's staff. Almost the entire company, to a man, had been disappointed when they learned of McKnight's return.

"At least Captain Brown would listen to us," said Gean in frustration. Gean was a seven-year veteran with four tours under his belt, including one in Iraq with the 1st Armored Division. Although he had served in Iraq and Afghanistan and had already earned his CIB, he never had a feeling of impending doom as he had on this patrol.

"Something bad is going to happen," he told Bleidorn.

The KOP LZ (photo provided by Bill Wilkinson)

The KOP LZ seen from O-P-1 (photo by Wilkinson)

(L-R) Jae Barclay, Adam Gordon, Parker Day (photo by Gordon)

(L-R) Neil Yusella, Bob Duncan, Chris Quinalty (photo by Quinalty)

"The Korangal was a bad place. This was my first deployment; I didn't know what to expect. We were in Khogiyani for the first three months. We were dealing with different elements, but the Korangal is different . . . some people compare it to Natrang Valley in Vietnam. It's desolate; people don't like you. It was just a rough tip of the spear . . . we were getting re-supplied all the time because we were going through so much ammo. Every third day we were getting hit. It was a tough place." Lieutenant Jae Barclay, 2nd Platoon Leader, A/1/32.

Waiting

Preston, Rush, and their 1st Platoon reached the Kandigal area at 0530, just before Morning Prayer. Everyone had been prepped about respect for the locals' religion and customs, so the patrol moved into position around the village and waited for Morning Prayer to end. When it did, Preston gave the order to commence the search of the village.

They cordoned the hamlet and sent the ANA in to search it. The villagers appeared to be frightened and wondered what was going on. The ANA and the intel personnel moved methodically from house to house, checking rooms and gathering information. Rush noticed most of the villagers were reluctant to speak to them or the ANA. They appeared to want nothing to do with them and resented the intrusion of having their village searched.

When the Americans asked for the village elder, no one responded. It appeared the village elder was either hiding or was not in the hamlet. Looking around, Rush could see the villagers going about their everyday lives. If there were enemy forces in the area, the locals either didn't know it or they weren't worried about it.

Preston called back to Attack Main and gave a SITREP while Rush and the others began checking around the village. They were waiting for the 3rd Platoon to arrive. In the meantime, they began trying to mingle with the villagers, buying Nan bread and Chai tea. They knew they were going to be in Kandigal for up to 72 hours, so they were trying to build rapport with the locals. The 1st Platoon occupied the village and had an element accompanying the Terp and the Intel guy as they went house to house talking to people. At the same time, the ANA were moving around, speaking with the villagers and seeing whether anyone looked suspicious. So far nothing was egregious.

The KOP; Hescos near the LZ: Duncan, Gean, Bleidorn, Quinalty, and Bratland sat with the others waiting for some type of word. There was still no sign of the ANA. The sun was slowly rising into the sky. Soon it would be hot. Everyone sat passing the time in their own way. Duncan sat beside Gordon. Like Bratland, Gordon wasn't part of the squad but was in the PL's HQ element. Whenever the PL went out, which was with every 2nd Platoon patrol, his element went with him.

Gordon and Duncan sat wisecracking everything from "Ass-crackistan" to their CO and MREs. The two had the sarcastic personalities in the group and took their humor seriously. That was possibly why they got along so well. Duncan was irrepressibly jovial while Gordon's humor was much drier. Gordon was quiet, but he enjoyed bantering with the always-laughing Duncan even though he considered the burly Iowan to be an out-of-control liberal.

Nearby sat Gean and Bleidorn. They talked about the good old days at the "Dexter" Manor back in Dexter, New York. It was the only thing that could keep Gean's mind off the feeling of impending disaster he felt looming. Gean and SGT Josh Lomen (age 25) of Longview, Washington, of the 3rd Squad, had a house out in Dexter. It was on the Black River, and they called it the Dexter Manor. Before they deployed, back in New York, whenever they weren't on duty, they were out at the manor waterskiing and drinking beer. Although Gean and Lomen owned the house, Bleidorn was their best friend and lived there with them. The three spent their downtime at the manor relaxing and hanging out.

Bleidorn remembered one drunken night when Lomen and Gean had left him asleep in their boat. They had pushed him out into the Black River and laughed as they watched him float downstream. Bleidorn had awakened to find himself in the middle of nowhere on the river without a key to the boat or even a paddle to steer the craft to shore. He was too inebriated to care much about it, and by the time he did, Gean showed up on a jet ski to tow him back. It was something about which they now laughed.

They both wished they could be back at the manor. But they weren't. Right now the two friends were thousands of miles across the globe in a valley in Asia waiting to head out on a combat mission. Gean still couldn't shake the uneasy feeling he had. It had been with him all morning.

LT Preston's Platoon; Kandigal: Having found nothing in the village, Rush ordered his soldiers to start searching the nearby farming terraces. Meanwhile, the ANA and Preston's Terp found an older Afghan that would talk to them. He was the first villager to do so. The man was not the village elder, but he would at least verbalize with them. Rush didn't speak Dari, Postu, or the local dialect, so he didn't know what was being said, but he could tell the ANA, their Terp, and the intel guy were trying to get a feel for the old man. He seemed friendly enough. Usually people were angry that they were in their village, but this man was not. They continued conversing, trying to get a read on him.

The KOP: There was still no sign of the ANA. Gordon sat wondering when they would finally leave. Gordon's two best friends in the unit were Gean and Bleidorn. He was still sitting beside Duncan and the others, waiting to leave. Gordon (who had no idea how Gean felt) was himself trying to fight a queasy feeling in the pit of his stomach. It had been growing. Gordon couldn't put a finger on it, but he felt extremely uneasy—so much so that he got up and walked over to the TOC where LT Parker Day was. Day was the company Fire Support Officer (FSO).

"Sir, I have a bad feeling about today," said Gordon bluntly. "L-T, will you stay in the TOC?" Gordon knew a SSG was on duty monitoring the radios that day, but if he needed incoming assets, he wanted Day in the TOC to make sure things went smoothly.

"Okay," replied Day.

Gordon then turned and sought out his friend and mentor, SFC Larry "Big Papa" North (age 43) of Mauk, Georgia.[vii] Gordon had a lot of respect for the five-foot-nine-inch, 160-pound North and asked his platoon sergeant to also stay close to the TOC. If they needed the QRF, Gordon felt North would get it to them as soon as was humanly possible. North said he would, and Gordon went back to the waiting group of soldiers.

Gordon sat down and leaned his tall body against the Hescos. He couldn't understand why they had been there all night. They could have waited in their tents. Then, they would have been rested. Now, it had been hours since the sun rose. If anyone was looking, and they were sure to be doing just that, they could see a group of soldiers waiting in full gear. Anyone looking from the high ground around them would know a patrol was waiting to go out. It frustrated Gordon to be powerless in the face of what he thought was idiocy.

LT Preston's Platoon; Kandigal: Preston and Rush wanted a location where they could establish security in the middle of the village and prevent the enemy access to it while they waited for link-up with 3rd Platoon. The THT operative and the Terp had been speaking to the same elderly Afghan. Preston had them ask the man whether they could rent an area in his village. Preston pointed to a spot that was centrally located, fairly secure, and shaded by trees. They asked whether they could acquire it as a safe house in the village where they could bivouac. The old man didn't appear to be very responsive to their request. He said that whenever people in the valley helped the Americans, it didn't look good for them. The ACM would target them. Since the Afghan hadn't said "no" outright, Preston had his Terp and the THT soldier keep trying. He hoped they could persuade him with the lure of money.

1130; ETT TOC: Hewerdine was finally notified by the ANA commander that eight Afghan soldiers were available to head south on a patrol. There would be an RPG team, an RPK team, and a PKM team with two AK-47-bearing soldiers. Hewerdine told Kraus to head for the LZ as the ANA commander said his troops were moving there now.

Attack Main TOC: Lieutenant Jae Barclay (Age 27) of Huntsville, Alabama, was in the TOC taking care of last-minute Pre-Combat Checks (PCCs) and going over details of his mission with North to make sure they had everything in order. They had done the checks in triplicate by now, but redundancy made for fewer mistakes. He also made sure he had extra batteries for his radio. Barclay was the 2nd Platoon leader, North the 2nd Platoon sergeant. Barclay was leading the patrol to Landigal; North would lead the mobile Quick Reaction Force (QRF) should they need one.

Also in the TOC were McKnight and SGT Blaine Stevens (age 31) of rural southern Maine. Stevens was McKnight's RTO. Stevens watched the patrol prepping to head out with mixed emotions. He knew Landigal was a bad place to go. They always had a TIC when they went there. He had been surprised when McKnight had gone down to send the men off with a prayer earlier that morning. The captain had never done that before. Even still, Stevens would have liked to have gone out with the patrol. Stevens was in the company HQ element against his will.

Stevens had originally been the RTO for a battalion commander and then a brigade commander, but he had asked to be transferred to an infantry platoon to get team leader experience. Only, when he got to A Company, McKnight had taken one look at his file and wanted him for his RTO. The position of RTO was extremely important, and a commander needed an able, competent soldier. Stevens had strongly requested he be allowed to serve as a team leader in a rifle platoon, but his request was denied. He had gone from being the RTO for a brigade commander to that of a company commander. Suffice it to say, he was very unhappy about it.

Interestingly, when McKnight had fallen off a cliff just over a month ago, most of the company swore it was Stevens who had pushed the captain. In fact, Stevens had been five feet behind McKnight when he fell. The fact that McKnight lived, that Stevens didn't spend the rest of his life in Leavenworth, and that he was still McKnight's RTO, did nothing to deter any of the soldiers from their belief on the subject. They were convinced the taciturn sergeant had given McKnight a shove.

Stevens was a very quiet individual. He watched more than he spoke, and he was well respected by the line troops, something not shared by all of those in McKnight's HQ Company staff.

McKnight spoke briefly to Barclay. They had already gone over the dual purpose of the mission, so there was no need to discuss it further. Barclay knew his commander was all about business. He never spoke to the captain any more than was needed. When he did, that led to strong conversations because McKnight, who was fairly new to A Company, would tell Barclay what should be done, and Barclay, who was the longest-serving officer in Attack Company, would have to deflect McKnight's order as much as he could to protect his men or talk the captain into what he thought was more prudent. That was difficult. Both men were strong-willed individuals.

Barclay turned and left the TOC, heading for his waiting patrol. Barclay was six feet two inches, 230 pounds, and extremely well respected by his soldiers. He was the 2nd Platoon leader, but on this patrol he wasn't taking his entire platoon. He was only taking out Gean's squad reinforced with an M-240B team. Lomen's squad would stay behind as the QRF, and Bleidorn's squad was on perimeter, although Bleidorn would accompany the patrol (because Gean was short a team leader). Their platoon was under strength to begin with as several soldiers were on leave. Everyone would have felt better if the entire platoon was heading south to Landigal.

Quinalty watched Barclay walk over and make a quick Pre-Combat Inspection (PCI) of the patrol. Gean had already done it, but once again, double and triple checking made for fewer mistakes. Satisfied his men had their weapons and gear in order, Barclay told everyone to ruck-up. They were finally moving out.

28

Quinalty thought very highly of his PL and was glad the LT was going on patrol with them. He thought Barclay was a great leader.[viii] Quinalty was a five-foot-ten-inch, 230-pound M-249 SAW gunner. He had big shoulders that helped him carry the eighty pounds of weapons, ammunition, water, and equipment he was taking on the patrol. Most of the weight Quinalty carried was his body armor, the full combat load of 600 rounds plus 200 in the drum, and three camelbacks of water.

They'd been sitting on the LZ all night, then all morning, and only now, at noon, did they appear to be heading out. With the exception of a short walk over to the "crap barrels,"[ix] none of them had been twenty feet from the LZ for the last eleven hours.

Quinalty looked around at the men in his squad and noticed Bleidorn was standing with them. That made Quinalty feel better, as he thought Bleidorn was one of the most squared-away soldiers he had ever met, right up there with Sergeant North and Sergeant Gean.

Quinalty remembered the first time he had met Bleidorn. He had just joined the company, and SGT Nat McKenzie brought him in to meet everyone. They were all together for an NCOs meeting—only Quinalty wasn't told that. Quinalty entered and began to meet what he thought were his fellow enlisted soldiers. He was showing the proper respect any new guy with brains would show, but he had no idea McKenzie was setting him up by bringing him into the lion's den of sergeants. He saw a man sitting back in his chair (Bleidorn) and approached to say hello. Quinalty couldn't see the soldier's rank, as the collar on Bleidorn's BDUs was turned up. Quinalty thought he was a specialist.

"Hey, what's up?" he said to Bleidorn. "My name's Q."

"Don't you fuckin' talk to me!"

Quinalty was new to the unit and thought maybe A Company was a prison-type environment where he needed to show right away he wouldn't put up with any crap.

"What the hell did you just say to me?"

Bleidorn shot out of his seat and got right in Q's face, saying, "If you ever fuckin' talk to me again like that, I will fucking kill you!"

Quinalty instantly saw the sergeant stripes and thought, "Oh no!" He immediately put his hands behind his back and stood at parade rest. Quinalty hadn't known that first meeting with the NCOs was a set-up, that they were testing him to see what kind of mental toughness he possessed, but from that moment on, he knew what kind of personality Bleidorn had. Quinalty had thought it was a bad start. However, Bleidorn proved to be an extremely professional NCO because he was instrumental in Quinalty's development as a soldier. In time, with a lot of errors on Quinalty's part, and patience on Bleidorn's, Quinalty felt he learned the right way to do things. He felt very confident when he saw Bleidorn was going on the patrol with them.

Lomen could see the patrol was preparing to head out. His two best friends in the company, Gean and Bleidorn, were the sergeants leading it. Lomen knew Landigal was out in the middle of nowhere, and every time they had sent troops there, they made contact. Lomen thought Landigal was probably the worst place in the valley, definitely and defiantly an enemy stronghold. It was also the farthest from support because the vehicles had a slow and dangerous route to get there, and it was a half-day's march on foot.

Knowing the patrol was most likely going to end in a TIC, Lomen walked over to Gean and said, "Dude, keep your head down. You're going to do the right thing. Keep your head on the swivel. Be the first to pull the trigger if necessary."

Corporal Neil Yusella (age 22) of Sioux Falls, South Dakota, was one of Gean's team leaders. Yusella turned to the three soldiers in his fire team and said, "We are going to a village where we expect to take fire. Landigal is a hundred percent contact rate. Be on the lookout."

Then Barclay gave the order for them to move out, and Bleidorn started down toward the road. Everyone else followed. More than one man looked at his watch as they left.

30

They were supposed to leave at 0100. When they finally moved beyond the KOP concertina wire, it was just after 1200.

"Attack Main, this is Attack Two-Six, leaving the wire now with thirteen Americans, eight A-N-A, one E-T-T, and two Terps."

"Roger, got it!"

Looking south from O-P-1 (photo by Wilkinson)

PFC Josh Caracciolo (by Caracciolo)

"It's obvious from anything you read: The Korangal Valley is the most dangerous place in Afghanistan. Landigal was the deadliest little village in the Korangal Valley. Every time we went there, we got hit; every single time, without question, it's a guarantee you're going to get shot at. One of our scouts got killed near there. That was Russell Durgin. We were in Bravo Company and served in Iraq together." Sergeant Adam Gordon, FO, A/1/32.

The Patrol Moves Out

On the map Landigal was only a few klicks southeast of the KOP. However, that was as the crow flew. Anyone who had traveled in the Korangal knew two klicks may as well be ten because of the steep mountains and unforgiving terrain. The valleys in the Korangal were steeper than most and at times shrouded in cloud cover. The added fact that they were infested with the enemy made rapid movement extremely difficult.

Bleidorn was on point with his Bravo Team of SPC Noli Ocompo, Duncan, and SPC Khuong Hang. Gean was next followed by Barclay's HQ element of the LT, his Terp, Bratland, their medic "Doc" Rob Marchetti, and their THT officer. Then came Gordon, followed by CPL Neil Yusella and his Alpha Team of PFC Josh "Crotch" Caracciolo, PFC Rueben Reyna, and Quinalty, for a total of fifteen men.

Ahead of them walked the eight ANA soldiers with Kraus, their ETT stand-in. The ANA hadn't been told where they were going. The patrol headed east-northeast down the KOP road.

The KOP; Prophet Element TOC: The US Prophet Team and their Afghan interpreter who were monitoring the frequencies used by the enemy picked up the first enemy "chatter" of the day. It was within minutes of Barclay's patrol's departure. The Afghan interpreter gave the information to the Prophet Element, and they quickly passed that information to Attack Main.

LT Preston's Platoon; Kandigal: Preston and Rush had not heard any ICOM throughout the morning. Then, just after noon the radio squawked with a message from Attack Main. The prophet element had picked up ICOM. The intercept reported a unit moving out of the KOP with ANA. Rush and his PL knew the 2nd Platoon had headed to Landigal, but Rush knew that patrol was supposed to have left hours ago. He wondered whether that was them. If so, they were delayed in heading out because now it was noon. If it wasn't them, Rush wondered what new patrol McKnight had moving.

LT Barclay's Patrol: Barclay's patrol wasn't 200 meters outside the wire when they received their first radio call. Bratland, Barclay's RTO, took the call from Attack Main on his ASIP and passed the information to his PL, even though the LT had already heard it on his own MBITR radio.

"Sir, ICOM just picked up 'Thirteen Americans have just left the wire heading to the southeast. The heavy machinegun is in the front of the column.'"

"Fuck!" muttered Duncan, who overheard. He carried the M-240B machinegun. It freaked him out to know he was being watched by the enemy right at that moment. It was nothing new. Every time he moved out on a daytime patrol since he'd been in the Korangal, they reported his position, specifically locating him in the formation within minutes of their leaving the wire. It made his stomach turn each time.

It was hot. Even though they were high in the mountains, the sun beat down on them. It was almost ninety degrees, and there was no breeze. Duncan had been walking for only several minutes, but already his pants and shirt were soaked. Per day they figured in about a liter to a liter and a half of water per man. Duncan carried three camelbacks of water—nine liters. The water was heavy. Of all the things Duncan carried, the water, the M-240B, and the ammunition were the heaviest. Duncan was learning to carry less and less food and began to rely on peanut butter as it was high in calories and high in fat, had protein, and packed the most punch for the amount of room it took up and the weight it added.

While the Americans were absolutely loaded like pack mules with ammunition and water, the ANA walked almost unencumbered. Although they had an RPG team, an RPK team, and a PKM team, aside from their ammunition (less than one-third the load the Americans carried), all they carried was a single bottle of water. They didn't wear body armor. This was because they didn't like to carry the additional weight. Needless to say, the ANA moved considerably faster than their American counterparts. The ANA thought the Americans were slow. The Americans thought the ANA lazy. These stereotypes were not singular to the Korangal but were a common belief held by both throughout Afghanistan—as was the belief held by many US soldiers that the ANA were notorious for avoiding the enemy.

LT Preston's First Platoon; Kandigal: Preston had gotten intermittent communication with the 3rd Platoon throughout the morning. The 3rd Platoon was making its way toward the Pesch River crossing for link-up at Kandigal. Then they would RIP (Relief In Place) to the KOP. Aside from that and the ICOM report, there had been very little radio traffic.

Meanwhile, the ANA continued meeting the locals. The Terp and the THT guy spoke to the old man. He was still the only local willing to speak. The THT was trying to find out whether the old man was someone from whom they could get information.

The THT looked almost like an Afghan. He was permitted to grow a beard and wear his hair longer. He wore traditional Afghan head attire that not only helped him blend in but also helped him generate cooperation. Big Army hated it, but it was essential to the Afghans. It was a way of showing respect for Afghan culture in hopes of earning trust. The THT hoped to find out whether the enemy was operating in the area. Preston's platoon had never spent time that far north, and they were trying to get a feel for the people. The general opinion was they were not welcome.

Preston and Rush again told their Terp to ask the old man whether there was an area they could take up as a safe house.

That way they could occupy and establish security in the middle of the village. The old man pointed to a building with a courtyard in an area of shade. It appeared to be pretty secure. The shade was something to which Rush and Preston immediately took a liking. The Korangal was heavily forested, but down by the river it was not. And it was already getting hot. The morning hadn't been too bad, but after noon hit the sun was high in the sky. They settled on a good price for the small compound, and Preston ordered his men to begin setting up a perimeter. They hoped at least a few people would be happy with the income their village had just generated. Maybe it would lead to valuable intel in the future.

Preston called back to higher and informed Attack Main they had rented two buildings with a compound overlooking the river. They began waiting around the village—trying to build rapport with the locals, and at the same time snoop about as much as they could without being obvious—while they waited for link-up with 3rd Platoon. The old man appeared to be someone with whom they could establish communications as he didn't seem at all angry they were in the village.

LT Barclay's Patrol: Bleidorn was almost to the point where they were to turn off the road and head south down into the valley toward the dry river below, when one of his soldiers called up to him. It was SPC Khuong Hang (age 25) of Chambersburg, Pennsylvania. Hang was five feet two inches, 145 pounds, and he carried more than half of his own body weight in weapons and ammunition. He carried an M-203 grenade launcher on his M-4 and had 36 grenades on him aside from his seven magazines, ruck, and two camelbacks of water. Hang was fatiguing.

Everyone was drenched in sweat, but Bleidorn was surprised someone was overheating so quickly. Hang was one of the new men to the Korangal. The others had acclimated to the ups and downs of valley travel, but the replacements had not adjusted yet—that and he was eighty pounds lighter than four of the other men on the patrol. But there was no going back. Bleidorn simply distributed some of Hang's ammunition and equipment to lighten the young soldier's load, and they started off again.

Bleidorn didn't say anything, but he was angry. Everyone was already loaded down like camels with almost eighty pounds of weapons, ammunition, water, and gear. Now they had a little more. He knew that humping the valleys was hard, but it was hard for everyone; you just did it and kept your mouth shut. Now, everyone in his team had extra weight. However, Hang was able to keep going.

It had been over an hour since Barclay's patrol left the KOP. The column made good time even though the terrain was rugged and difficult. They had only been in the Korangal since mid-July but had already gained needed stamina because of all the patrolling they had done. They worked their way down along a goat trail heading for the riverbed far below.

Bratland descended the steep valley and remembered the first day they flew into the Korangal. It was 14 July. The 2nd Platoon had not been with the initial A Company platoon (1st Platoon) when they arrived at the end of May. The 2nd Platoon had been in Khogiyani, a flat area of desert surrounded by mountains. When the 2nd Platoon finally got orders to rejoin the rest of Attack Company, they had flown in on Chinooks in the middle of the night. Bratland had been asleep but was wakened when someone said, "Dude, this is bad!"

Bratland had felt the big Chinook moving fast and winding back and forth. It was black as pitch out, so he put on his night vision and went to look out the back of the bird. All Bratland saw were trees on near-vertical cliffs seemingly no more than fifty meters from the Chinook. Bratland couldn't see the tops of the valley walls, only steep cliffs that went up and up.

"Holy crap!"

Bratland was from the plains of South Dakota. He saw the near-vertical mountains and thought they looked like pictures he had seen of Mount Everest as a kid. He leaned his head up and out to try to see the tops of the mountains, but all he saw was valley going up. The helicopter wound back and forth through the gorges, and several of Bratland's fellow ground-pounders were vomiting. Bratland could feel when the big

Chinook hit a thermal draft because the aircraft rose and fell each time.

"Good God, no!" he thought. "This isn't going to end good no matter how we do it. This is bad!"

Now, it was twenty days later, and Bratland had humped up and down more hogbacks, spurs, switchbacks, and ridgelines then he ever cared. He still wasn't used to the steep mountains.

They reached the valley floor and crossed the Korangal River. In the winter it was frozen. In spring and fall it was a fast-flowing river with rapids. In the heat of summer after the snow melt, it was bone dry.

The patrol started south on the east side of the riverbed at the bottom of the valley, plodding along. They were maybe halfway to Landigal, having traveled for over two hours, when they came upon a small village that was not on their map. That was not uncommon. There were villages all over the valley, some nothing more than seven or eight mud huts along the side of a mountain. It was below Donga, which was higher up on the side of the ridge. Barclay decided to conduct a cordon search of the village for dual reasons: First, they were asserting themselves in the area and wanted the locals to see the ANA controlled the valley, and, second, they did not want to possibly leave a hostile enemy directly to their rear when they pushed on.

Barclay called Kraus and the ANA patrol leader over and told them what he wanted. Since he obviously didn't want the ANA with their ETT to enter the village until his soldiers were in position to protect them, Barclay set a time and had Kraus and the ANA leader coordinate their watches to his.

Meanwhile, Gordon called back to the KOP and got their 120 mortars laid on likely targets, should the enemy hit them during the search.

Once everyone knew the plan, Barclay told them to execute. Barclay's soldiers climbed the valley and got into over-watch on the ridgeline above the village. They were attempting to remain unseen. Then, at the coordinated time, Kraus and the ANA entered the village and began searching the buildings. Barclay, Bratland, their Terp, and the THT followed them in. Bratland saw several of the villagers looking at them and thought they were some of the most anti-American people he'd ever seen. They glared at him and the others. Bratland felt if they could have shot bullets out of their eyes, they would have.

The search didn't turn up anything that indicated an enemy presence. Although several of the Korangalis had AK-47s, there was nothing for which the ANA could detain them. The law allowed one weapon per household, be it an old flintlock rifle or and AK-47 assault rifle. That was very disconcerting for the Americans because many times it seemed they would pass through a village and then be fired upon by the same AK-toting Afghan who had been smiling at them minutes before.

After the search, the ANA continued on, and Barclay had Gean move his soldiers down to link up with them beyond the village. They were now three quarters of the way to Landigal and on their third hour of marching. The ominous village was maybe 1,000 meters ahead as the crow flew, but because of the winding, snaking valley, they couldn't see it.

Yusella, one of Gean's team leaders, was confident his team would do well. They had never seen combat before, but they were solid. Quinalty was one of his soldiers. Quinalty was Yusella's work horse. The big Texan carried most of their weight because he was physically bigger and stronger. Yusella was five feet five inches and 170 pounds. He carried as much ammo and water as he could. The other soldiers in his team were around his size. But Quinalty was 230 pounds, and he was strong as an ox. Yusella knew the big Texan was a good soldier, too. The only bad thing was Quinalty needed more water than the rest of them because he was pushing more weight all the way around. They were all bathed in sweat, but it looked to Yusella as though Quinalty had just gotten out of the shower, as he was sweating so profusely in the heat. Caracciolo was another soldier in his team. Caracciolo didn't look nearly as imposing as Quinalty, but Yusella knew he was also a good soldier. Caracciolo was lean, but he could road march and run with the best of them. He was also very motivated. Yusella liked that he was an easygoing, stand-up guy who never got in trouble.

The patrol continued on. They moved deeper to the south keeping their eyes on the eastern and western ridges. There was nothing different as far as anyone could tell, but most everyone began to get that strange feeling that something wasn't right—that uncomfortable eeriness that soldiers would get just before combat.

Since 10th Mountain troops had been in the Korangal, three times they had pushed south into the Landigal area, and three times they had kicked up a TIC. In June, Scout Sniper Russell Durgin had been killed when his six-man sniper team was ambushed. Gordon had known Durgin fairly well. He had served in the same company with him in Iraq.

Gordon thought it had been asinine to send six men out by themselves to be ambushed, but he wasn't in command.[x] Gordon understood the idea behind the scout sniper teams, but in the Korangal they didn't work unless they were inserted carefully without being seen, usually after they broke off from a main group. But still it seemed the enemy always had eyes on. They outnumbered any small unit that moved out. And the enemy always held the high ground. Gordon and the others knew that mountain warfare was all about holding the high ground. American soldiers were heavily laden with body armor and equipment. It was always easy for the enemy to get high ground on them because the ACM wasn't as heavily weighed down—that and most of them had grown up in the mountains. They could move through the valleys like mountain goats.

The eeriness Gordon had felt earlier returned. He scanned the valley sides and set TRPs on likely spots from which the enemy might try to ambush them. Then he called back to LT Day and had the 120s registered on those TRPs.

The patrol continued on. Bratland felt that had they not had the ANA with them, they would already have been hit. Then they came upon a local. The man was walking toward them. He was moving north; they were moving south. The ANA stopped the man, and Barclay's Terp asked where Landigal was. The Korangali pointed down the valley and spoke.

40

The very moment the ANA heard "Landigal," it appeared to the Americans that they bristled.

"Oh man," thought Hang, "this is going to be bad." Hang didn't know anything about Landigal and didn't even know where it was, but when he saw the reaction of the ANA, he thought to himself, "Something's going to go wrong."

The Korangali continued on his way north while Barclay ordered the column to press on to the south. The patrol kept moving, but it was obvious the ANA were suddenly very edgy. That made the Americans nervous. Everyone knew the Afghans had an almost-innate sense when it came to ambush. Although none of the ANA felt comfortable in the Korangal, and seemed nervous all the time, they still knew the country better than anyone outside the valley. And whether or not the Americans thought they were cowards, it couldn't be denied: They seemed to know there was going to be trouble. Now even the Americans felt it. There had been an almost-palpable change in the air, but it was just a feeling. Nothing could be seen or heard that was out of the ordinary.

The KOP; Prophet Element TOC: There had been no enemy ICOM since the initial report that the patrol had left the KOP. Suddenly the airway came alive with a message. Viper Two-Five's Afghan interpreter intercepted the enemy communications: "They are heading for Landigal."

Viper immediately passed the information to Attack Main.

(L-R) Dan Hewerdine, Chuck Martin, Nate Kraus, Dennis McClain
(photo by Hewerdine)

Nick "Scrappy" Bratland in Khogiyani (photo by Bratland)

"Every time we went out, they had guys watching us. They had spotters up in the mountains watching us, guys with just a radio—just to sit there and say how many guys are leaving the wire. Their radios were not encrypted like ours. We started going; we're in a riverbed. The ANA start to make up a bunch of excuses. 'We can't do night missions. We don't have enough food and water.' We told them we'd give them water and buy them food. They said, 'Our commander says we can't stay out here.' They left us high and dry. We needed 'em to stay, but they left, and there was nothing we could do. They left, and McKnight wanted us to push on. You have a company commander making calls like this? I don't mean to talk bad about anyone, but you have people back there that know what is going on, and they don't have the balls to step up and say, 'Hey sir, you need to bring those guys back.' The first sergeant or someone should say, 'Hey, get those guys out of there.'" Sergeant Chase Gean, Squad Leader, 2nd Platoon, A/1/32.

The ANA Bug Out

It had been only ten minutes since they had asked the local where Landigal was when everyone on the patrol with a radio heard Attack Main give the latest report: "Viper Two-Five reports enemy ICOM: 'They are heading for Landigal.'"

"Fuckin' great!" thought Bratland. "They know right where we're going." The patrol was moving through the river bed maybe four or five fingers from where Durgin was killed several thousand feet up the mountain.

The Americans were alert. The ANA were extremely nervous. They seemed to be walking much more slowly, as if very reluctant to continue. Suddenly the ANA patrol leader walked over to Barclay and spoke to his Terp.

"We need to go back. We need to go back. This is a bad place."

Bratland stood near Barclay and thought, "Typical A-N-A, they're scared shitless. They don't want to put one foot in front of the other."

"We have orders to cordon search Landigal," said Barclay.

"We need to go back. This is a bad place."

43

When the ANA were nervous, the Americans knew to possibly expect a TIC. Barclay got everyone stopped and put out a security element. Gordon called back and gave a grid, laying the 120s at the KOP on the surrounding valley walls with TRPs in each direction maybe 300 meters in diameter around them. He wanted the tubes pointed in the right direction to reduce the reaction time from minutes to seconds. If they got hit, he could have 120mm fire support within thirty seconds. It was something Gordon did constantly, and the others marveled at his ability as an FO.

Barclay called a leaders' huddle with the ANA patrol leader, Gordon, Bleidorn, Kraus, and Gean. The two Terps were there as well. Being the RTO, Bratland stood beside Barclay. None of them wanted to be there. It was obvious from the enemy ICOM that their destination was known. Barclay had been able to keep good coms with Attack Main all afternoon, but he had lost them in the dry riverbed. He assumed the steep valley prevented him from getting coms on his MBITR. He told Bratland to get the long antenna up on his ASIP and turned back to the other three. He reiterated their orders to get to Landigal and asked his NCOs whether they had anything.

"Sir," said Gean to Barclay, "if we lose the A-N-A, we can't stay out here." Gean knew if they lost the ANA, things would go from very bad to much worse. They had been walking for almost five hours, and that alone meant they were out too far for any dismounted QRF to reach them quickly. Any mounted QRF would only be able to support them from the road high above them on the side of the valley.

Gean noticed no one was trying harder to get the ANA patrol leader to stay than their Terp. The young Afghan was pleading for his fellow countrymen to stay. It didn't work. The ANA patrol leader was resistant to anything other than heading back to the KOP. The Americans tried to get their fellow American, Kraus, to persuade the ANA to stay, as Kraus was the ETT stand-in. They felt Kraus, who was very young and mild mannered, gave a halfhearted attempt that only got weaker through translation because Kraus's Terp wanted no part in staying either.

The ANA patrol leader looked terrified. He went over to his soldiers, and they had a quick meeting. He turned to Barclay and said they were heading back to the KOP. He said he and his men were going to go back with or without the Americans. He advised the Americans to turn back with them.

Bratland had the long whip (antenna) up and told Barclay his ASIP was working, and he had coms with Attack Main. Barclay called back and told McKnight the situation.

"The A-N-A want to bug out," said Barclay. He told Attack Six what the ANA patrol leader had said and added, "This is what we are being told. If they turn back, I'm not comfortable pushing my guys further with only us here."

The KOP; Attack Main TOC: When Barclay asked for permission to turn back, both McKnight and Dales had the same thought at the same time. Both men knew Barclay was an able and brave commander, but they also held the opinion that Barclay would forget about the mission when it risked putting his soldiers' lives in danger. Since there was not a safe place in the Korangal, any mission was a dangerous mission. Both McKnight and Dales remembered a time before when Barclay had called back and said his men couldn't complete their mission because it didn't look good to him as commander on the ground. McKnight had let him return the time before. Now he was asking again. McKnight ordered them to push forward to Landigal.

LT Barclay's Patrol; between Donga and Landigal: Yusella wasn't surprised when he heard McKnight's order for them to stay on mission. He knew before the answer came back, there was no way their CO would let them return to the KOP. Yusella felt McKnight would not hesitate to send any of his men into harm's way but would never go himself. He remembered McKnight's prayer the night before and thought, "You should be out on patrol with us."

The ANA leader went over to his men and started giving orders. The ANA turned back to the north and started moving toward the direction of the KOP. They had been leading the patrol, so they had to pass back through the Americans. Barclay stepped in front of them with his Terp, determined to try to get the ANA to stay. He reminded the ANA patrol leader of their mission and his duty as a soldier.

"We don't have enough food and water," said the Afghan.

"We'll give you some. We got plenty of food and water," said Barclay. The Americans were carrying double food and water. This was the first time Attack Company had ventured south, and since they didn't know what they might encounter, they had prepared for the worst. They had extra everything to allow for all contingencies. "We have iodine tablets to get more water if we have to," added Barclay.

"We need to pray," said the Afghan.

"We will stop so you can pray."

"We don't have our prayer mats."

From the front of the column where he was pulling security, PFC Joshua "Crotch" Caracciolo (age 19) of Lancaster County, Pennsylvania, heard the Terp translate that last one and thought, "Crap, they are lying. They just don't want to do this." Then he heard Barclay say, "We need you to stay on mission."

"Our commander says we can't do night operations," said the Afghan. "We don't have night vision."

ETT TOC: Hewerdine had been in coms with both Kraus and McClain throughout the day. He had just gotten off the radio with Kraus. The young specialist had given him a SITREP, and both men knew the ANA were right. Viper had already reported the enemy had eyes on. It was an ambush waiting to happen. Then Hewerdine got a call from Attack Main. They were requesting Hewerdine get the ANA commander to order his soldiers to remain on mission. Hewerdine said he would do what he could. He headed over to the ANA TOC.

The ANA TOC and the ETT TOC were very close. It was designed that way because the ETT needed to have access to the Afghan commander he mentored. Hewerdine entered the TOC and greeted his Afghan counterpart, CPT Mohd Zman. He asked the ANA commander whether he'd been keeping abreast of the situation. Zman said he had.

"Look," said Hewerdine. "Tenth Mountain needs those guys to stay on mission. Can you call your guys and tell them they need to stay out there?"

"Dan," said Zman, "I have a limited number of men. It is a bad tactical decision to leave my men there. The enemy knows they are there. The enemy is above them. They are waiting for them."

It was hard for Hewerdine to argue against the man. As a commander, Hewerdine saw his point and knew he was right. If they were his troops, he would get them out of there. And, because he was an ETT, the ANA were theoretically his troops. Against his will, he had to keep trying.

"Yes, I understand, but Tenth Mountain needs them to stay."

LT Barclay's Patrol; between Donga and Landigal: The Attack Company soldiers again turned to Kraus, trying to get the ETT fill-in to appeal to the soldiers he mentored. It seemed to them the SPC tried halfheartedly to talk the ANA into continuing. It was obvious, though, he had absolutely no control over the ANA. Beside the fact that Kraus was mild mannered and mellow in personality, he was a teenager, not even twenty years old. All the ANA were much older than he was. In Afghan culture, age went far. Kraus didn't even have facial hair, something the Afghans saw as wisdom and ability.

Caracciolo kept his eyes on the nearby cliffs. He was worried about an ambush. Caracciolo was five feet nine inches and 150 pounds. He stood at the head of the column along the left side of the riverbed. Reuben Reyna (age 19) of Whittier, California, was opposite him on the right side. Yusella and Quinalty were behind them about five yards. Caracciolo was leaning against the side of the mountain, looking up to the left. He faced left, and Reyna was supposed to face right. Only, when Caracciolo glanced to the side, he noticed Reyna was also facing left.

Caracciolo used two fingers to point at his eyes and then pointed to the right; then he pointed at Reyna. He felt a tinge of exasperation when Reyna pointed at him and repeated the motion, indicating that Caracciolo was supposed to do it. Caracciolo again made the hand signals and pointed, trying to tell Reyna to turn the other way. Reyna again signaled back, telling him he was wrong. The two continued their silent struggle. Soon their hand signals began to get harder and more intense. Caracciolo pumped his arm in frustration trying to get Reyna to look to the right.

"No," said Reyna angrily, "you guard that way."

"No," said Caracciolo forcefully, "you do!"

Quinalty was watching the cliffs, but he was still listening to LT Barclay as he tried to talk the ANA into staying on mission. He could also hear Caracciolo arguing with Reyna. They always seemed to argue. Quinalty thought they were like a married couple the way they constantly quarreled. And the arguing seemed to always be the same. Caracciolo would start it by telling Reyna to do something. The Hispanic American would refuse and say he was going to do it differently. The Italian American would respond angrily that Reyna needed to do it the other way, and Reyna would respond with an insult, usually about Caracciolo's mother, which would send the mellow specialist into a smoldering fury.

Quinalty had grown close to Caracciolo since he'd joined the company. Quinalty almost always referred to his friend as "Crotch" because it was easier to say than Caracciolo and because the only time he actually used Caracciolo's first name, he got chewed out by McKnight. They were in a HMMWV with their CO when Quinalty called Caracciolo "Joshua." McKnight had reprimanded him and said it was unprofessional for soldiers to be on a first-name basis. Quinalty and Caracciolo had laughed about it later because they knew each other better than that, but Quinalty never called anyone in his company by their first name again. Now, standing in a dry riverbed on their way to Landigal, Quinalty pulled security but listened as his friends bickered.

"YOU guard that way," insisted Reyna.

"NO! You do!"

Yusella, their team leader, heard the two arguing and hissed, "What's all the commotion?" Then he noticed that Caracciolo wasn't looking in the direction he was supposed to be looking and was instead looking at Reyna. Yusella snapped, "Why aren't you facing that way?"

"I am," said Caracciolo, "but Reyna keeps looking left. Nobody's watching right. I was trying to get Reyna to look right."

"You're supposed to look right," said Reyna from across the riverbed.

"Whatever," said Caracciolo, knowing they were giving away their positions with their arguing. "I'm not going to listen to this." He turned back to the left and pulled security. He heard Yusella walk over to Reyna and start talking quietly to him. Then Caracciolo heard Gean come up. Their squad leader seemed mad and asked Yusella what was going on and why they were making noise. Yusella told him, and Gean snapped at him to keep them quiet. Then he went back to where Barclay and the ANA were.

First Platoon; Kandigal: Preston and Rush spent the day waiting. They periodically called back to the KOP and gave SITREPs to McKnight and acting 1SG North—telling them what the situation was, giving them updates.

"Attack Six; Attack One-Seven."

"Go ahead, Attack One-Seven."

"So far, this is what we've got in the village. The village elder is not here. We've spoken to a number of people. We compiled a decent sketch of the village. Right now they are not really completely agreeing with us, welcoming us with open arms, but they are also not misleading us. That is my general feeling."

"What do you think about possibly supplying the village with H-A goods?" asked McKnight.

"Let me get a little better feel for the village before we go ahead and launch the stuff up here."

"Yeah, okay," said McKnight, "sounds good."

It was a short conversation. It was just after 1700. After Rush gave his report, Preston had everyone start to move away, so the villagers could do their evening prayer. The ANA stayed so they could pray and talk to the villagers and continue working at building rapport.

ANA TOC: Hewerdine was still talking to the ANA commander. Several messages had come from Attack Main requesting the ANA stay with Barclay's patrol. Zman had never said "no" outright; he was just stalling. Hewerdine was angry at the position in which McKnight had placed him. He was trying to convince his ANA counterpart, a man with whom he had been trying to build rapport and trust, to do something he knew was tactically unsound and, in Hewerdine's opinion, downright stupid. If the troops were Hewerdine's, the Viper intercepts alone, not to mention the small size of the force, would make him bring them back in.

On top of that, Kraus was under Hewerdine's command. The lieutenant thought it was unconscionable for him to ask Kraus to stay out in what would probably result in an ambush. And the ANA troops, although they were not American, were also Hewerdine's responsibility. He had been out on patrol with them and had built camaraderie. Now he was asked to keep them where the enemy had eyes on them. Hewerdine was at a loss. He hated the situation, and Zman was still stalling.

The KOP; Attack Main TOC: McKnight called back to battalion HQ. He spoke to the BC about Barclay's predicament.

"Sir," said McKnight, "the A-N-A are threatening to leave Second Platoon. If we lose the A-N-A, theater S-O-P states we can't cordon search an Afghan village without them. Do I pull Barclay's men back?"

The BC told McKnight that regardless of what the ANA did, he wanted the 2nd Platoon to stay on mission.

LT Barclay's Patrol: It had been an entire hour since they first stopped, and Barclay tried everything to parley with the ANA patrol leader. Quinalty was listening as the Terp relayed the questions and answers back and forth. Finally the ANA leader turned to the Terp and said bluntly, "The enemy is waiting. We have no reason to go forward. We are going back." Then he turned, gave a quick command to his men, and the ANA started back to the north.

The Americans watched them walk away in a mixture of anger and trepidation—anger because many of them thought the ANA were cowards and trepidation because they knew they had just lost considerable firepower. Gordon had felt something bad was going to happen. Now he was convinced of it. He watched almost half their combat power leave and felt a sickening feeling in his stomach. Instead of there being 24 guys for the enemy to fire at, now there were only fifteen including the Terp and the THT. Barclay got back on the radio to call Attack Main.

"The A-N-A are gone. They headed back to the KOP." Barclay stated that their numbers and firepower had just been significantly reduced. Barclay was very direct and blunt: "We need to come back. This is not a good idea." He again asked permission for his patrol to return to the KOP.

The KOP; Attack Main TOC: McKnight and Dales were in the TOC with Stevens, Day, and North.

"Continue mission," ordered McKnight. "Do not turn around. You can handle it with the guys you have."[xi]

LT Barclay's Patrol; North of Landigal: Quinalty heard their CO's order to remain on mission and wasn't surprised. To the burly Texan, the order was like all McKnight's other orders, "given straight down without due consideration or thought."

To Bratland, Barclay was visibly livid when he got off the radio. Bratland had never seen such a look of fury on the LT's face. He heard Barclay mumble aloud to himself, "What the fuck are we supposed to do? We get hit, we don't have enough guys to fight."

Bratland thought Barclay was the finest officer he had ever known and felt his CO was furious with Attack Six. However, because he was so professional, Bratland knew Barclay would never say something about another officer in front of his men. In fact, Bratland had never heard Barclay say anything negative about anyone. Bratland remembered the first day the LT came to their platoon and addressed all the soldiers together.

"Hey guys, I'm the new P-L. This is my first year. I know that you've been through the war in Iraq and the past two P-Ls got relieved. I'm here to change that mentality you have for your P-Ls. I'm going to rely on the N-C-Os' and the platoon sergeants' leadership because they've been leading you guys a lot more than I have. Hopefully we will become a well-oiled machine."

To Bratland, that's how Barclay was as a leader. Even if he thought he knew exactly how it should be, he would consult his NCOs—the guys who had been under fire before. He would hear their input before making his decision. Bratland had the utmost confidence in Barclay.

Bratland saw Barclay looking around, as if he was trying to figure out what to do. He scanned the high ground, as if he was looking for a place to stay the night. It was getting into late afternoon, and it was going to be dark within two hours. Bratland wondered whether they would push on through the night or whether they would hunker down.

"Fine," thought Barclay. "I have to continue mission; I'm supposed to set up an ambush. The best possible way to keep my guys safe is to set up a defensive position. I'll still achieve the mission, have eyes on the riverbed infil and exfil, and be able to bunker down for the night." He decided right there they would find the most defensible position they could and button up. They would move on to Landigal in the morning.[xii]

Barclay consulted with Gean, Bleidorn, and Gordon again. He reiterated the situation as he knew it. He explained to them what they were being told from higher. Barclay told them how he felt and said, "I think we should find some high ground and bunker down for the night. What is your input on this?"

The consensus of his NCOs was very cut and dry. Get to the highest ground as fast as they could, get a perimeter up, and dig in. Everyone felt that eerie, something's-not-right feeling.

Barclay spoke quickly to his NCOs. He consulted his map and told the others there was a spur that jutted out into the riverbed about 100 meters ahead around the next bend. He told them he wanted to move quickly to that spur and get on it in over-watch. Everyone concurred, and Gean gave the order for Yusella to get Caracciolo and Reyna moving again. He called back to Attack Main and told McKnight he would move to a spur a few hundred yards ahead and set up their ambush position.

The patrol covered the next hundred meters with their eyes on the valley walls and their weapons ready. They expected a TIC at any moment.

The KOP; Prophet Element TOC: Viper Two-Six continued to monitor the airwaves. They picked up the latest ICOM: "The Afghans have turned back. The Americans are alone. Hit them hard. Hit them the way we taught you"

They immediately passed the information to Attack Main.

ANA TOC: Hewerdine was still talking to the ANA CO when Kraus radioed that he and the ANA were on their way back. They were almost to Donga. Kraus explained what happened. Hewerdine got off the radio and headed back to the ETT TOC.

The KOP; O-P-Two: Brown was up near the O-P-2 60mm mortar pit. The east Texan was a five-foot-nine-inch, 170-pound graduate of West Point and had been the Attack Company commander for the last month while McKnight convalesced. Now that McKnight was back, Brown didn't have anything to do and was just waiting for CPT Marc Blum's Easy Riders to arrive on 6 August bringing supplies. He would then hitch a ride back to Jalalabad with Blum's convoy and rejoin BN.

Brown was BS-ing with the guys at O-P-2, absentmindedly listening to the radio. All over the KOP everyone had them on. They couldn't help but overhear what was going on. Brown had been loosely following the day's chatter, but he was taking more interest in it now that things seemed to be turning disturbingly for the worse. Brown couldn't understand why the patrol had been ordered to remain on mission. He got up and walked down to the TOC. He was powerless to do anything, but he wanted to know what was going on.

LT Barclay's Patrol: The 2nd Platoon soldiers rounded a bend and came upon the spur Barclay had mentioned. It looked to be defensible and provided good over-watch of the riverbed. The spur was very steep and covered with holly bushes with sparse trees. A short distance away was what looked to be a goat trail that led all the way up and around to the top of the spur. Barclay had a decision to make. "Do we go straight up the side of the spur, or do we take the goat trial?" he thought to himself. "Do they have eyes on us? If they don't right now, if we take a hard right and go straight up, maybe we'll lose them and catch them off-guard on the other side."

Then Attack Main sent the latest Viper intercept. It made everyone who heard it turn cold with fear: "The Afghans have turned back. The Americans are alone. Hit them hard. Hit them the way we taught you."

Gordon immediately called back and laid the 120s in a 300-yard radius around them. Every 10th Mountain soldier in the Korangal knew they weren't just hitting a bunch of farmers with assault rifles. They were fighting professional soldiers taught to fight by leaders with extensive experience fighting the Russians—some of whom were taught by the CIA over twenty years before. It was also possible they were fighting against the very terrorist leaders who had planned 9/11.

Barclay quickly consulted with Gean, Bleidorn, and Gordon and told them he thought it would be best to move straight up the spur to try to get to the top as quickly as possible under the cover of the vegetation. If they went the easier route, it would take them longer, and they would

54

undoubtedly be seen. He asked for any reason that they shouldn't go straight up. His sergeants didn't have any. Barclay gave the order, and everyone started up the steep embankment. He hoped they might disappear from the eyes of the watchers and actually get surprise on the enemy. He hoped to be able to ambush whoever was following them. In a spread-out line, the fourteen Americans and one Afghan Terp pushed up the side of the incline.

The KOP; Second Platoon Tents: SGT Shane Wilkinson (age 22) of Saint Louis, Missouri, was sitting in his tent with SPC Pat McClure (age 22) of Waynesburg, Pennsylvania, and several other soldiers including SGT Eddie Hernandez (age 23) of Washington, D.C. Everyone was waiting with their gear on because they were the QRF. Whether they would head out on foot or go out in the trucks usually depended on the enemy, but both attack elements were now so far away that any QRF would have to be mounted. It seemed to Wilkinson the ICOM traffic indicated they would probably be moving fairly soon. Then Lomen popped his head in the tent and said, "Willie, Herny, have your teams ready."

"Roger that," said Wilkinson. They already were.

The KOP; Attack Main TOC: Brown entered the TOC and walked up to Stevens and Day. He asked what was going on. They told him what he already knew from listening to the radio chatter.

"Why won't he let them come back in?" asked Brown.

"Battalion's pushing it."

Brown was frustrated. He left the TOC and headed back to O-P-2. There was nothing he could do. He had hated losing command of Attack Company. These had been his men. Now he was watching them get placed in an extremely dangerous situation. Brown had not liked the sound of the mission since the moment he heard about it. He knew the force they sent to Landigal could never have isolated it and searched it properly. Brown remembered when they took a patrol to Darbat. He had accompanied it. They had Preston's entire platoon along with almost twenty ANA—over fifty men—and they still didn't have enough soldiers to successfully cordon it. The enemy filtered out of the village on the sides they couldn't block off. They had more than three times as many soldiers at Darbat, and they couldn't do it. Brown thought about Russell Durgin and hoped history would not repeat itself.

Durgin had gone with a small unit, six men, into the same area just north of Landigal. Durgin had been killed when he inadvertently walked into an enemy ambush. Durgin's patrol, too, had been out with the very purpose of ambushing the enemy. Brown hoped Barclay's men would be okay.

Brown thought about what Stevens and Day had said: "Battalion's pushing it." In Brown's opinion the BC interfered and micromanaged his companies way too much. He hated it. Now, from Jalalabad, Brown felt the BC had McKnight refusing to allow his men to come in because battalion had a clearer picture of what was going on—clearer than Barclay or McKnight. Brown felt it was asinine.

It reminded Brown of a training mission at the National Training Center at Fort Irwin, California. While on maneuvers, playing war games, CPT Mike Mulherin had gotten into a skirmish with the OPFOR (opposing force). He was told that before he could get certain assets, he had to take X number of notional casualties. He then took fire from a ridgeline. BN got CAS on station and told Mulherrin to pull back. BN wouldn't pass the aircraft to him and controlled a notional CAS bomb drop. Only, the CAS caused one notional fratricide. Mulherrin then went back in and took more notional casualties but finally defeated the OPFOR. Brown had been part of BN staff at the time, and the actions of their TOC disgusted him.

During their AAR, nobody mentioned what happened and how the TOC quantified the use of an asset with the deaths of US soldiers. Brown had stood up and said, "I have something to say." He was told to go ahead. Brown described what happened and said, "Battalion has no business questioning a commander on the ground. It's wrong to quantify the use of an asset with the deaths of American men. The commander on the ground has the clearest picture of what is going on, and the TOC should not question him and instead should support him."

The BC had become angered and said, "You are exactly *wrong*, Captain Brown!" Brown heard the BC explain how the man on the ground didn't have the clearest picture and that the TOC could better understand the fight and direct it. That was not what Brown had learned at West Point. Now the same thing was happening, and the same BC was micromanaging it, but this time it was for real, not some maneuver in California.[xiii]

Back in the TOC, Dales was working with McKnight, Stevens, and the rest of the company staff. Dales felt the situation was uncomfortable whenever Brown and McKnight were in proximity. Both men wanted command. The men wanted Brown and did not like McKnight. But McKnight was their CO. Dales felt almost sick about it because the men showed no loyalty to their commander. He remembered when they had first heard that McKnight was returning to the KOP several weeks before. Brown had gathered all the company NCOs together to make the announcement. There had been a collective sigh from almost the entire tent full of men when they heard Brown say McKnight was returning. Some of the sergeants openly cursed aloud in anger. Dales thought, "Where is the loyalty?" He likened it to someone cheating on their wife. He thought the sooner Brown went back to BN the better. While they were both at the KOP, it would only cause tension and make things harder for McKnight.

LT Preston's Platoon; Kandigal: Preston and Rush heard the latest ICOM reported by Attack Main. The last message meant someone was about to be hit. Rush didn't think it was going to be his platoon. The ICOM didn't match up with what they were doing. Although Rush felt their coms were somewhat hazy because they were constantly bouncing back and forth between 3rd Platoon and 2nd Platoon, he was pretty sure the ICOM meant bad news for the 2nd Platoon.

If it was his platoon, Rush wondered from where the enemy might hit them. The first thing he did was look across the river to the high ground on the opposite side. One thing Rush knew for certain was that the enemy knew how to make use of the terrain. Very rarely could the Americans close on the enemy. The enemy was always putting the valley between the two forces, so they could expend their ammunition (inflict their damage) and then get away. Since fighting in the mountains was all about who could get to the high ground the fastest, and since it was a lot easier to move in "man-jamis" than in ACUs and body armor, the enemy always dictated when, where, and for how long they were in contact. Very rarely did they ever stay and fight. The enemy broke contact when they wanted to.

Rush had served in Iraq, as well as Afghanistan, and couldn't help but contrast the two. They were two completely different types of warfare. Rush felt war in Iraq had been a lot more up-close and personal. In Afghanistan, they never saw the enemy. They were like ghosts.

ANA seen moving down the riverbed (photo by Zuzzio)

Another view of the riverbed (photo by Zuzzio)

Khuong Hang taking a breather with his squad (photo by Hang)

Duncan taking a breather (photo by Lomen)

Alia Bad (left) and Donga (right), ANA in foreground (photo by Zuzzio)

Typical Afghan terraced village that caused difficulty to cordon and search
(photo by Lomen)

(L-R) Chase Gean, Chris Quinalty, Josh Caracciolo in Khogiyani (photo by Gean)

Chase Gean in Khogiyani (photo by Gean)

"Captain Barclay (lieutenant then) was a soldier's soldier [and] officer who knew his responsibilities were to accomplish the mission and see to the welfare of the men. He shared in the hardships with the lowest-ranking private. He always asked for the N-C-Os' input and was a methodical thinker who had both outstanding tactical sense and just downright good common sense. As a young lieutenant with no prior combat experience, he matured very quickly and always led from the front without hesitation, showing no fear. He instilled confidence in all the soldiers, and he never asked any soldier to do anything he would not do himself. I was proud and honored to serve next to a warrior of his caliber."
Sergeant First Class Larry North, 2nd Platoon, A/1/32.

The Climb

The ascent up the spur was exhausting. They had covered maybe 100 meters and had 300 more to go. Each soldier was loaded down with one third of his own body weight in weapons, ammo, and water, and everyone was already tired from six hours of humping rough terrain. Some men were slipping on the steep incline and sliding back down the hill. Others would take three steps forward and slide back two as they tried to keep their footing.

It was very steep, almost seventy degrees in places, and never fewer than 45. The dirt was soft and would give when stepped on. Barclay and Quinalty were 230 pounds. Bleidorn was 220, and Duncan was just as big. They had the hardest time as the dirt constantly gave beneath them. Everyone used their hands on the slope in front of them as they climbed. Bratland watched Duncan slip several times and slide back down, once almost ten feet.

"If we get hit here," thought Gordon as he struggled with each step of his long legs, "we can't do a thing about it. If we get hit now, we'll all be slaughtered."

There were holly bushes everywhere. It was hard for anyone to put their hand down because the leaves were hard and pointy. Gordon thought they were almost like kabobs. And they were everywhere. Gordon had to keep his gloves on, or he'd rip his hands to shreds while he climbed.

Quinalty was bathed in sweat. When he had arrived at the Korangal, he was 241 pounds. He was now down to 230 and he hadn't even been there a month. He couldn't shovel MREs down fast enough to replace the spent calories. He was exhausted and hungry and hoped to be able to eat soon. Even more, he wanted water. He had to stop and drink water constantly. He feared when it would run out.

Yusella climbed with his hands on the ground ahead. The side of the spur was so steep that it was as if he was bear-crawling; only, he was still in an upright position. He had already slipped and fallen back several times. He was using trees and branches to pull himself up and keep from sliding back. Yusella was tired and wondered when they would reach the top. It seemed the spur had several false tops. He kept climbing, watching the others slipping and falling around him. He saw Hang slip and fall, but the Vietnamese American caught himself after sliding back five feet. Then Ocompo fell. Everyone was either losing their grip or pulling roots out of the ground, falling to their face in front of them. In the midst of this instability, Yusella was thirsty. Everyone was drinking water. Yusella drank and worried about not having enough. He knew they had a limited supply.

Hang saw SPC Noli Ocompo of Manila, the Philippines, climbing off to his side. They were in a spread-out, faltering, sliding line working their way up the hill, but Ocompo had gotten away from them. He accidentally climbed up on a rocky extension of the spur that was slippery and came to a ninety-degree face. He tried to move to the side, but Ocompo was on his belly and suddenly began sliding back. He called out for help to keep from gaining momentum. Hang saw that if Ocompo fell, he might slide back thirty or more feet onto rocks below. Hang started sideways toward him. Ocompo's hands were slipping on the rocks as he struggled to grab anything. Hang reached over, and Ocompo grabbed his hand just in time to stop his slide. But Hang had no leverage. He was stretched out and trying desperately not to fall himself. He hugged the rock face for all he was worth while Ocompo snail-crawled over the rock to him. Then he slid over Hang's body to get back to the 45-degree cliff face. Once both were safe, they began climbing again.

Caracciolo was spent. "When will we finally reach the top?" he wondered. It seemed they would never stop climbing. He was hungry. Even more, he was thirsty. Caracciolo was trying not to drink too much for fear of when it might run out.

The climb was a nightmare. Everyone tried to move with a sense of urgency, but it still took almost an hour for the patrol to make it up the 400 meters to the top of the spur. They were on an outcropping directly above the riverbed. There were two spurs on the far valley that jutted out toward them on both their right and left as the river wound through. The opposite spurs were only 300 meters away. It was very disconcerting to know the enemy might have eyes on them at that very moment.

When they hit the top of that ridgeline, Barclay was breathing as though he'd run a marathon. Even still, he wasted no time. He turned to Bratland and said, "Scrap, get Sergeant Gordon, Sergeant Gean, and Sergeant Bleidorn; get them up to me now. We need to get shit happening. We need to get set up now! I've got coms on my MBITR. You need to get coms up." Bratland had never seen Barclay so intense.

While Barclay was issuing orders, Gordon was getting a hold of the guns. Before the climb he had adjusted them to where he thought the enemy attack might originate, where they could best support someone on the floor of the valley. Now he had the 120s laid on a higher elevation on the opposite valley, 300 meters away from them where he thought they might get hit at their present position. Then Bratland told him Barclay wanted to see him. Bleidorn and Gean were there, as well. Barclay wasted no time.

"This is what I want," he snapped, pointing to a nearby grouping of holly bushes. "I want the two-forty here; I want the two-o-three there. Get these guys set up; get a perimeter. I want three men in each spot, five meters apart." He explained their length of fire and gave their target directives: "Get the crickets and the strobes up. If we get slammed and have to call for fire,

Sergeant Gordon, I want Target Reference Points for the artillery, predetermined, written down, ready to go."

Bratland listened and thought, "I've never seen the lieutenant so shit-hot on what he wants done."[xiv] Bratland was getting the long-whip antenna set up as the lieutenant finished his briefing with, "That's how it is; don't ask me any questions, just do it."

Barclay turned to Gordon and reiterated, "Make sure we have targets up."

"I'm on it," replied Gordon. He had already done it.

"Scrap," said Barclay as he turned to Bratland, "you got the radio up yet?"

"Yes, sir, but I can't get any reception." Bratland had the antenna up but couldn't raise anyone. Their position in the steep valley prevented his ASIP from getting reception. He moved to another spot but still couldn't reach anyone.

"Keep moving," said Barclay. "Find someplace on this damn mountain that gets reception." Barclay wanted redundant communication in case his MBITR failed. It was working fine, and he had coms with Attack Main, but he wanted Bratland's ASIP up, too, just in case.

Dusk was maybe thirty minutes away. Even though they had climbed for an hour, there was still higher ground. The patrol was on the side of a ridge where the enemy could get on top of them. That was what everyone feared most.

Yusella was lower down on the spur with his team: Reyna, Quinalty, and Caracciolo. Yusella didn't like the look of the open area in which the others appeared to be setting up and told his men to get lower in better cover. Yusella pointed at a position even lower on the spur and said, "Q, get down there."

Quinalty had the M-249 SAW, and his primary directive was to lay down a heavy base of fire—what the Texan called "Scunion." However, Quinalty took one look at the position and felt his combat intuition warning him against it. He turned to his team leader and said, "Corporal Yusella, can I talk to you?"

Yusella exhaled in what Quinalty knew to be annoyance, but he walked over to the specialist and allowed Quinalty to speak.

"Listen," said Quinalty in his slow Texas drawl, "I don't feel right sitting down there. Wouldn't it be better if I covered this open area here?"

"Fine," said Yusella in irritation, "but I'm going to talk to you when we get back." Then Yusella turned to Reyna and pointed to the spot: "Get down there." Reyna did.

"Sergeant Gean," said Hang, not liking the position where they set up, "we need to take some cover. Get behind some trees and bushes."

"I know," said Gean, pointing to some nearby cover higher up. "Move over here."

Bratland found a spot that enabled his ASIP to work. Unfortunately, it was in an open spot on the spur with no cover for almost fifteen meters. Not only was it in the open, but Bratland also had to hold his radio pack on his back just to get the antenna up high enough to get coms with Attack Main. The spot was in the middle of their perimeter.

"Sir," he said to Barclay, "I got 'em."

Satisfied they were in as defensible a position as they could find, Barclay turned to his soldiers and said, "We got twenty minutes. If you're hungry . . . eat. Do it now 'cause you aren't getting a chance again for a while." Then he moved into the clearing with Bratland and Doc Marchetti.

Hang was highest up the spur. He was responsible for anything coming in behind them. He looked around and did not like the position in which some of the others were set up. There was cover around them; they just needed to utilize it better. Hang looked to the south down the valley and saw Landigal and the little village just before it. He couldn't see movement in either.

Caracciolo was lower down, but he, too, could see Landigal. He didn't see anyone moving either. He knew that was never a good sign but hoped it was because the Afghans were at prayer.

The KOP; Prophet Element TOC: Viper intercepted: "We've got three enemy soldiers on the curve at checkpoint three out in the open."

They sent it immediately to Attack Main.

LT Barclay's Patrol; North of Landigal: Barclay didn't need Bratland's radio to talk to Attack Main, but he was glad of the additional coms. He called back on his own MBITR.

"Attack Six, Attack Six, Two-Six Actual, pause goes as follows, prepare to copy grid." He gave their grid and waited for just a moment before Attack Six responded: "Roger. Copy. Be advised, Viper Two-Five has caught ICOM traffic. The enemy's exact words were, 'We've got three enemy soldiers on the curve at checkpoint three out in the open.'"

Bratland felt his stomach drop. He, Marchetti, and Barclay were sitting out in the open on the spur above the riverbed. But there was nothing they could do. If they moved, the radio wouldn't work. Barclay wasn't convinced the ICOM was in reference to his patrol. The 1st Platoon was up near Kandigal. Maybe they were being monitored. He remembered hearing something about them setting up in a courtyard and thought the report was being called on them. And even if it wasn't, the three of them were still in the middle of their perimeter. He felt they were as safe as they were going to be.

LT Preston's Platoon; Kandigal: Preston and Rush received the same ICOM transmissions. Rush looked around at their positions to see whether he had three men in the open. The building on their left had a little courtyard. The building on the right was elevated from the road. It was probably eight feet higher than the road. Rush knew the enemy had high ground on them, so maybe they were looking at his men in the courtyard.

"Shit," thought Rush, "unless you're up on Abbas Ghar or Divpat, it is easy for them to get the high ground." From almost any direction he observed the enemy would be able to see them. There were several people in the courtyard, but Rush also saw some of his soldiers moving to and from O-Ps—a lot more than three. He figured the enemy must be talking about 2nd Platoon.

LT Barclay's Patrol; North of Landigal: Bratland looked across the valley at the spur 300 meters away. It was still light, and he could see into the trees on the opposite side. He felt if anyone was moving through the trees, they could see them.

Everyone was in position and hunkered down. They had three 3-man clusters and two 2-man teams in a cigar shape along the spur with the Terp and the THT in the middle. Each cluster was roughly five meters apart. Dusk would come soon, and everyone expected contact. Barclay got off the radio and racked his mind for any last-minute preparations. He lay prone several yards from Bratland and Marchetti. They were still sitting in the little clearing because they dared not move for fear of losing coms. Everyone broke open an MRE. Security was up, and everyone was already in their rotation. It was still twenty minutes before they would go to 100 percent security until an hour after dark.

The KOP; Second Platoon Tents: McClure, Wilkinson, Hernandez, SPC Miguel Salano of Mexico, and several other soldiers on the QRF sat waiting. Everyone had heard the radio traffic, and both Lomen and North had told their men repeatedly to be ready. Everyone expected the worst.

"I can't believe he would send that few people to the most dangerous place in the valley," said McClure. "If you are going to send a mission up there, send two or three squads with A-N-A. Why send thirteen people?"

Everyone was in agreement. There was a lot of negative talk about McKnight.

LT Barclay's Patrol; North of Landigal: Caracciolo was close to Reyna, about five meters to his right and a little farther up. Ocompo was above Quinalty, maybe five meters up from him behind a rock. The Philippino was sitting quietly. Quinalty was in a little area of trees and bushes all by himself.

Caracciolo could just see him, but he hadn't heard a sound out of Quinalty since they set up their perimeter. Caracciolo felt that was because Quinalty was such a good soldier.

Duncan had his weapon pointing down the river valley towards Landigal. He had the only heavy machinegun, so he was in a position with the best angle to hit from the twelve o'clock to the six o'clock. Up above Duncan, on the very top was Hang. He and Ocompo defended the top of the spur. They were all expecting contact to the south-southwest. They covered ten o'clock to two o'clock. The 203 gunner always covered the dead space of the 249 SAW or the M-240B, the greatest casualty-producing weapons in the platoon (after Gordon's radio). Everyone covered ten to two in their direction. A soldier's ten o'clock field of fire intersected someone else's two o'clock position. That was a kind of fail-safe point. If the enemy got past that point, it meant big trouble.

Gean and Bleidorn were next to each other, about ten feet from Duncan. Gordon was on the flat part of the perimeter, a smooth rock area. The spur dropped down, and that was where Yusella's team was. Their perimeter wasn't much more than thirty meters. They had the crickets out and the IR strobe lights to demarcate their lines. They were as ready as they were going to be.

"It's about time when they've been hitting us," said Bratland to Barclay and Marchetti, looking around. It was the eeriest feeling Bratland had ever known. He felt like throwing up. Usually when he humped unforgiving terrain he was famished and hungry. Now, he had no appetite and ate only because he knew he had to. The eeriness was so intense that he'd never known anything like it.

Bratland scanned the opposite spur. There was no movement that he could see, but the terrain was thick with holly bushes and trees. It was still light, but it wasn't going to stay that way for very long. He couldn't hear anything, and that in itself lent to the eeriness. Usually birds or insects were alive with chatter, or monkeys could be heard rushing around among the small trees. Now nothing could be heard. The air was heavy with silence.

Everyone was eating. Duncan and Bleidorn smoked. Bratland felt everybody wanted to but worried the smell would give their positions away. It was still light out so they didn't have to worry about a glow signature. Once night fell, the smokers would be unable to strike up until first light tomorrow. That was why guys like Bleidorn carried chewing tobacco. He would smoke by day, chew by night.

They were on the edge of the spur above the riverbed with 280-degree low ground. Only the area behind them, above Hang and Ocompo, gave the enemy high ground on them. The riverbed below looked to be maybe 200 meters across. That indicated how steep the valley was because the opposite spurs were only 300 meters away, and they were at least 400 meters up.

Bratland looked down from their position and sized up their situation. With the nose of the spur being their twelve o'clock, they covered the river below from their nine o'clock to their six, maybe six-thirty. If the enemy came at them from anywhere but behind them, they would be able to put up a pretty good fight.

Barclay's patrol was in a 360-degree perimeter. At the end of the night, when they would collapse their perimeter, Barclay and Gordon would move into the center of the cigar, and that's where they would stay, being the PL and the FO. Normally the RTO would stay right with the lieutenant, but Barclay needed every man he had defending the edge of their perimeter, so once they went into full security, Bratland would move out.

Gean was so hungry he had the shakes. He tried whipping up some Ranger pudding—water and cocoa. He was listening to the ICOM chatter on his own radio. Their Terp was within five meters of him listening as well. Gean could tell the Afghan was extremely apprehensive.

"That guy's shitting bricks," realized Gean nervously. "What are they saying?" he asked the Terp. The young Afghan was visibly sweating, and not from the heat. He said he could pick up only bits and pieces because they were using a

71

Korangali dialect. The Terp's frightened eyes constantly scanned across the valley as he continued to listen.

The KOP; Prophet Element TOC: Viper's Korangali-speaking Terp picked up what Barclay's Terp could not understand: "Start the countdown. Let's hit them when it's dark."

Viper immediately sent the message to Attack Six.

LT Preston's Platoon; Kandigal: Preston and Rush were both listening to the radio when Attack Six relayed the latest intercept: "We just picked up, 'Start the countdown. Let's hit them when it's dark.'"

"Okay," thought Rush. "We're going to know soon enough whether it's us or Second Platoon."

LT Barclay's Patrol; North of Landigal: Barclay had just been getting ready to eat something when he heard the same message Preston and Rush heard. Barclay dropped his MRE and headed for the closest three-man cluster to warn his soldiers of the latest intercept.

"Sergeant Gean, Sergeant Bleidorn, and Sergeant Gordon got hit about the same time. All the sergeants were hit so the leadership right there was gone except for me. It was pretty chaotic when you get hit like that; your squad leader, your team leader, and your FO are all shot. Sergeant Gean was the guy who held everybody together. SGT Gordon was shot in the foot, but he was still calling fire. It was pretty cool how he was able to handle the situation being shot like that. Gordon was great; probably the best FSO in the brigade.[xv] I was pretty lucky to have him." Lieutenant Jae Barclay, 2nd Platoon Leader, A/1/32.

The Spur

Bratland watched his PL stoop to warn the nearest cluster of their latest ICOM. Then Barclay moved to the next group. Bratland had never been more afraid in his life. He had been forcing himself to eat because he knew he needed the calories. He finished as much of the meal as he cared to and pulled out the dessert. It was his favorite, brownie and chocolate chips. Then, to Bratland, the unthinkable happened.

"Hey, let me have that brownie."

It was Marchetti, calling over from his spot a few meters away. He wanted the brownie and chocolate chips out of Bratland's MRE.

"Not gonna happen, Doc."

This had been one of the worst days of Bratland's life, but it was bearable if he could just have the brownie and chocolate chips. It had always been his favorite and the one thing he counted on to make life bearable in the Korangal.

"Come on," said Marchetti, "lemme have the brownie!"

Bratland could tell Marchetti was serious. He really wanted his brownie. He wanted it badly.

"Ain't fuckin' happenin'. Shove it up your ass. This brownie is my one damn joy in this shithole, and you ain't gettin' it."

"Just gimme the damn brownie!"

"Doc, if you try to take that brownie, I'm punching you in the fuckin' throat."

73

"I'll beat yer ass, Bratland!"

Just then Barclay returned. He dropped down hissing, "Why don't you split the damn thing in half and shut up?"

First Platoon; Kandigal: Specialist Randall Carter (age 18) of Nashville, Tennessee, was standing atop a roof in Kandigal looking to the northwest. The rest of the platoon and their ANA were spread out, just sitting or standing around, occupying the site. They were on the left side of the road facing north.

Carter was the FO for the 1st Platoon. He was on the roof because he was looking for any sign of the enemy, and the roof gave him the highest vantage point in the village. He had laid in several TRPs just in case. Carter turned toward the river when several shots erupted from the trees to the south, some 300 meters across the river. In an instant, numerous AKs opened fire, and at least one RPG and a PKM machinegun.

At the first *pop*, Carter was moving. He took one step toward the edge of the roof and dropped ten feet down to the ground below. He didn't care if he hurt his ankles; he just wanted defilade from the incoming rounds. Carter landed hard but rolled and came up running for cover. The gunfire was deafening as the 1st Platoon responded instantly. Every weapon that could be brought to bear hammered back at the tree line from where the enemy fire emanated. Preston and Rush were instantly on their MBITRs calling Attack Six.

"ATTACK SIX! THIS IS ATTACK ONE-SEVEN! YOU'VE GOT TROOPS IN CONTACT! STAND BY; FIRE MISSION WILL FOLLOW!"

Rush couldn't see any muzzle flashes, but he knew from where the bullets were impacting what direction the fire was coming from. It was the high ground across the river. He searched for any sign of an enemy position so he could call in mortar fire.

LT Barclay's Patrol; North of Landigal: Barclay and Bratland heard Rush calling in the TIC over their secure net.

"It was them after all," thought Bratland. He breathed more easily. He felt bad for the 1st Platoon, but he was grateful it wasn't 2nd Platoon that got hit. Kandigal was maybe ten klicks away, but Bratland swore he could faintly hear the sound of distant gunfire.

Yusella had all his men in position and was walking over to Gean to inform him where everyone was. He was maybe fifteen meters away from him.

Gean watched the sun go over the top of the mountain. Bleidorn was listening to his radio. Then he heard their Terp report the latest ICOM. The Terp said he overheard the enemy give grid coordinates. He didn't understand what they were saying because they were speaking Korangali, but numbers were very similar, and those he understood. He said he heard, "Two hundred fifty degrees."

Bleidorn pulled out his compass and checked his map.

"Hey," he said to Gean, "that's right over there. Two hundred and fifty degrees is right there." Then there were several loud *swoosh* noises, and it sounded as if the southern Korangal exploded. Gean felt a sharp pain in his back simultaneous to the sounds of roaring gunfire.

"What the hell just happened?" thought Gean, stunned. He had been sitting, but now he was lying prone. It was as if someone walked up and slammed him in the lower back with a sledgehammer.

Both Bleidorn and Duncan had been looking at Gean. To Bleidorn it looked as though Gean's lower back exploded. Duncan saw blood spurting out. The sound of dozens of weapons firing at once thundered in the valley. The enemy was also firing multiple RPGs because explosions erupted one after another.

"MEDIC!" shouted Bleidorn as he scrambled for cover. "MEDIC!"

"GET TO THE OTHER SIDE OF THE SPUR!" roared Duncan as he jumped up and ran for better cover.

Yusella was almost to Gean when the gunfire ripped apart the silence of the valley. Yusella didn't think; with bullets slamming everywhere around them, he just reacted. He did a

75

superman right off the side of the spur. He was in midair with his arms out, falling.

Bratland's brownie went flying into the air. He forgot about his radio and went for his M-4. When the enemy opened up, he hit the trigger.

Barclay had never heard anything like what enveloped his unit at that moment. No live fire exercise or firefight to date had even been so violent. For just a moment he was awestruck by its fury. Barclay's MBITR was rigged to his mouth. All he had to do was touch a button on his chest, and he could speak into his radio. The gunfire and explosions thundered, and he was calling Attack Main.

"BREAK! BREAK! TROOPS IN CONTACT! TROOPS IN CONTACT! MULTIPLE ENEMY ELEMENTS!"

Gordon had been eating crackers when the gunfire started. He had no idea what happened to his crackers and simply hit the trigger.

Duncan vaulted to the other side of the spur and swung his M-240B around. He pounded one of the spots where fire was originating.

Yusella landed maybe fifteen feet below from where he had jumped. He scrambled back up toward his position to control his fire team.

The KOP: It seemed to the soldiers in the KOP the entire south valley exploded with gunfire. McKnight heard the firing and thought, "Hey! Jae kicked off the ambush, and we got 'em!" He immediately gave the order for the QRF to head out. He wanted to make sure they killed as many as they could. North was already moving out of the TOC.

That same moment, at the QRF tent, McClure was sprinting outside, his weapons and assault pack trying to keep him from moving fast. He raced for the vehicles. Right behind him were Wilkinson and Hernandez followed by Salano and the rest of the QRF. At full sprint McClure saw North emerge from the TOC heading for the vehicles. North was waving everyone down, trying to hurry them to the HMMWVs.

Hewerdine had been in his ETT TOC listening to the radio. Kraus still wasn't back yet, although he had radioed he was close. At the eruption of gunfire Hewerdine grabbed his rifle and ran out the door of the ETT hooch. He saw Dales across the helipad, hurrying the QRF. Dales was McKnight's XO. Hewerdine ran to within earshot and shouted, "I'LL GO ON THE GROUND!" Then he took off running for O-P-3, the southernmost ANA position at the end of the KOP spur.

LT Barclay's Patrol; North of Landigal: Caracciolo had an M-4 with an M-203 grenade launcher. He was halfway through a mag when he realized his grenades would be much more effective than his M-4. He switched to the M-203 and saw Reyna firing at a cluster of rocks in the trees across the valley. Every third round Reyna fired was a tracer. Caracciolo lobbed a 40mm grenade at the rock cluster. He could hear Quinalty's SAW firing in short, controlled bursts. Yusella was just climbing back up to them.

Bratland didn't quit until he burned through a mag. He slapped another in and went through it just as fast. Bratland could see muzzle flashes everywhere. The enemy opened up on them from their two o'clock to their ten o'clock.

Gordon went through a mag and a half before he realized, "Wait a minute, I need to get on my radio." He jumped behind a holly bush and got his compass to call in a fire mission. Gordon was sitting on his heels, squatting and trying to keep his six-foot-six-inch frame as low as possible. He looked down and saw dust kick up between his feet, right by his genitals. Suddenly he felt an intense pain, as though someone had just hit his heel with a hammer. The shockwave went right up through his groin.

"I just got fuckin' hit!" he said to himself in surprise. Then he felt the pain in his testicles.

"Oh my God! I just got shot in the balls." He frantically checked his groin for blood or any sign of a wound. There was none. His genitals were fine; it was his heel that was shot.

"Okay," thought Gordon, regaining his composure. "I can deal with this." But Gordon suddenly realized, "I'm not in a good spot. Someone can obviously see me. I'm not as well hidden as I think I am." He moved on adrenaline and ran back for the other side of the spur.

Hang could see Landigal and the small village just before it. The enemy was firing from the small village. A round hit beside Hang, maybe five inches from him. The tracer came from the village. Hang aimed a 203 round right at the building from where the shot had come. He hit the small hooch dead center, and it exploded into flame and black smoke.

Gean was lying prone looking back down his body. He couldn't understand why his body wouldn't respond. He was trying to get up but couldn't. He tried to see what was wrong with his legs, but all his gear obscured his vision. Gean could see his midsection in a pool of his own blood. He reached down with his hand to feel his legs, and it was as if his heart froze. Gean knew what it was like to pick up a dead body. They were limp and had no muscle tone. He felt his legs and went cold with fear. He could feel his legs with his hands, but he wasn't feeling his hands with his legs.

"My God!" he said to himself. "I've been blown in half!" He had heard the RPG blasts and knew they hit close. He wondered where his legs were severed and felt for the amputation. Only, his legs were still attached to his body. That was when he realized he was paralyzed. Bullets were punching into the ground around him, ricocheting off the rocks. Terror enveloped him, and he began screaming for help.

"SOMEBODY HELP ME! I CAN'T MOVE! I CAN'T FEEL MY LEGS! HELP ME!"

Gordon heard Gean screaming and looked over to see his friend lying in blood with bullets impacting all around him. Gordon had only heard that kind of urgency in a human voice once before—in Iskanvariyah, Iraq, in 2004. Their base had received devastating mortar fire, and half their tents were burned down—with seven soldiers killed and twice that wounded from horrible burns when their anti-tank rockets and ammunition cooked off. Gordon had tried to put out the raging fires, but the extinguishers were dead. In desperation he had thrown several extinguishers into the flames in hopes they would explode and smother the fires. The same urgency of burning soldiers' pleading for help was the tone Gordon heard in the screams of his good friend Chase Gean. His buddy was lying in the open with bullets kicking up all around him.

"HELP ME! SOMEBODY HELP ME!"[xvi]

For Gordon to reach his friend, he would have to run across open ground, then stoop and pick him up under a hail of fire. Gordon wanted badly to help his friend, but he didn't want to die. More importantly, he knew they all might die if he did not get fire support immediately. He had to make the excruciating decision not to help his friend.

"ATTACK FOUR-ZERO! THIS IS ATTACK TWO-ZERO! IMMEDIATE SUPPRESSION! POLAR DIRECTION ONE FOUR ZERO MILS; DISTANCE THREE HUNDRED METERS!"

Within thirty seconds of the TIC, Gordon had the 120 mortars slamming the opposite spur where the enemy fire was originating. Since he already had the guns laid in on target, he gave directions for LT Day to start walking the explosions in a crescent shape around them. Gordon was on a separate radio net talking to Day. That way he wouldn't be stepping on Barclay's toes as the LT communicated with McKnight at Attack Main.

Bratland burned through a third mag, firing faster than he ever had in his life. Barclay was beside him, firing just as fast. Incoming slammed the ground around them.

"There's no way I'm going to survive this," thought Bratland. He had never seen so many muzzle flashes in his life. Bullets were snapping by them.

"GORDON?" yelled Duncan. He had seen Gean get hit and now worried Gordon had been shot, too. Bleidorn was off to his side hammering away with his M-4. Duncan didn't see the FO anywhere and didn't hear an answer. There was roaring gunfire and RPG explosions seemingly everywhere.

Gean tried crawling, but his legs wouldn't work. He had so much gear on his arms that he couldn't pull the combined weight of his body with almost eighty pounds of water and ammunition. He was unable to get himself to cover. The enemy kept targeting him with their machineguns. Bullets were kicking up all along his body, ricocheting off the rocks near his face. More terrified than he'd ever been in his life, he realized he couldn't do anything. He couldn't even help himself.

Then something slammed against Gean underneath his armpit. He figured it was a rock thrown from an explosion or a piece of shrapnel. Suddenly a rage boiled up inside him as he realized he was defenseless, and they were still trying to kill him. Screaming in pain and rage, he grabbed his M-4 with one hand and started hammering back at the enemy. However, he couldn't bring his other arm over because his body wasn't responding, and he couldn't get the leverage to get both arms to the gun.

Bratland could hear Bleidorn bellowing, "GEAN'S DOWN! GEAN'S DOWN! TWO-TWO'S DOWN! TWO-TWO'S DOWN!"

Then Bratland remembered the radio.

"ATTACK MAIN! ATTACK MAIN! TWO-SIX ROMEO! TROOPS IN CONTACT! BREAK!"

Bratland saw rounds impacting in the clearing all around him. The enemy had them dead in their sights.

"Time to go," he thought. Bratland had his M-4 in his left hand and his antenna in his right. He started low-crawling up the hill back to the trees. Marchetti was right beside him. Rounds were chasing them as they crawled.

"MEDIC!" shouted Bleidorn. "GEAN'S DOWN!"

"FUCK THIS!" said Marchetti as he got up and started running. Only, Bratland was surprised where he was running. Marchetti wasn't heading for the cover of the holly bushes ahead. He was running toward Bleidorn. Bratland could see rounds going everywhere. The enemy was firing tracers, and they knifed by the medic as he ran.

Bratland kept low-crawling as bullets flashed over his head or kicked up around him. He looked up and saw Barclay hurtle over him. The LT stopped just inside the cover of the trees and turned to open fire. The lieutenant saw Bratland and didn't think he was moving fast enough.

"FUCK THAT, SCRAPPY! MOVE GODDAMMIT!"

80

"Screw you," thought Bratland. "I'm going as fast as I can."

Barclay was hammering back at the enemy when Bratland got to the edge of the trees. Only, he couldn't push through. They were too thick, and he couldn't crawl through with his radio on. Bratland had grown up hunting in South Dakota. When he needed to get through thick brush but couldn't push through, he just rolled over on them. Then, he'd fall back and roll off as they snapped back, and he'd be where he wanted to be. He tried that on the holly bushes, but it was like hitting a concrete wall. Bratland fell on his butt, surprised.

Duncan couldn't see from where the fire was coming. The flash on his M-240B was blinding him. "I can't see shit," he thought in frustration. He saw Bratland stuck against the nearby bush and yelled, "HELP ME IDENTIFY TARGETS!"

"THEY'RE SHOOTING AT YOU!" Bratland's tone said what he was thinking, "Are you fucking blind! They are everywhere!"

Duncan still couldn't see any muzzle flashes, but rounds were impacting on both sides of him. They were also hitting the ground ahead of him and going over his head. Duncan slid down a little farther to the side of the spur for better cover. Barclay shouted over at him, telling Duncan where to shoot.

Gean was still firing. Bullets were kicking up all around him. The enemy wanted him dead. But either the enemy were really bad shots, or God just did not want Gean yet. By now several empty magazines were lying beside the wounded sergeant. That was the hardest thing for Gean, reloading. He had to reach down his body, fish out a mag, replace the old mag with a new one, and then bring the M-4 back up. He had to aim and fire with one arm while incoming ricocheted around him.

Gean suddenly became aware of the sound of explosions. They thundered in the valley. One-twenty mortars were slamming into the far ridges. That was how Gean knew Gordon was still alive. Then Gean felt someone grab him. It was Marchetti. The medic stooped down and pulled him. Marchetti began dragging him away. It was not going well. Marchetti was small in stature, maybe 160 pounds. Gean was 190 pounds, not including his heavy equipment. Gean tried to help, but his legs weren't responding. Bullets rained down around them.

Bleidorn watched the medic pulling his friend and tried to lay down covering fire. Duncan was rocking with the M-240B laying down even more suppressive fire. Bleidorn marveled at how Duncan was able to spin that weapon around and fire it when he needed to move fast. Bleidorn could hear Gordon adjusting fire on the 120mm mortars as they screamed in to explode on the opposite valley. The firefight was only a few minutes old.

Duncan and Bleidorn were hammering with their weapons when they received a massive burst of fire from at least one PKM. Both men dove sideways. Bleidorn dove to the right, Duncan to the left. Bleidorn felt a hammer-like force hit him below his armpit. It felt as though someone slammed him hard with an intense punch and took his wind. He felt underneath his arm for blood but didn't find any. He crawled behind a tree maybe two inches in diameter, hoping it would give him some cover, and resumed firing.

With nowhere to go and bullets hitting around him, Bratland blew through another magazine. Every flash he saw he tried to return fire in that same direction. He had an M-68 red dot on his M-4, and he would put the dot just above the muzzle flash and start squeezing rounds. He had stacked his mags so that every third round was a tracer. He also had one full mag of tracers because as an RTO it was possible he would be talking to Fire Support. He was on that magazine now. He tried to help Duncan find targets, but at the moment he was more concerned with saving his own life. The incoming was intense. Bullets were passing everywhere around him.

"I'M STUCK!" yelled Bratland. "HELP ME GET OUT!"

Bratland was surprised when Duncan reached through the bushes, grabbed the back of his ruck, and shouted, "BRATLAND, DON'T LET GO OF YOUR FUCKIN' GUN!" Then Duncan yanked him back through the trees. Duncan was big. He was a stereotypical, corn-fed farm boy from the Midwest, built like an ox. Bratland's whole body came off the ground when the Iowan pulled him. As soon as Bratland was over the bush, Duncan went prone and started blazing again.

"Thank God for this big motherfucker!" thought Bratland. "He just saved my life." Bratland upped with his M-4 and started firing again.

Barclay wasn't sure who was hit, but he knew someone was calling for a medic. His mind was moving at warp speed trying to do everything at once. He was firing his weapon and only stopped long enough to call back to let Attack Six know they had wounded.

"WE'VE GOT CASUALTIES!" He had to shout over the roaring gunfire to be heard. "STAND BY!"

"Who's hit?" asked Attack Six.

"WAIT ONE!" said Barclay.

Barclay was engaging a cluster on their west side. The cell appeared to be possibly five enemy soldiers supporting a PKM machinegun. The incoming was intense.

"We need battle roster numbers," said Stevens.

"WAIT ONE!"

Duncan was rocking on the M-240B when he felt something pass over the top of his leg. He looked back down his body and saw Bratland right beside him, firing across his leg at a new threat.

"We are all cluster-fucked in here," realized Duncan in fear. If he had shifted to get up, Bratland would have inadvertently shot him in the leg. Duncan wanted to move away, but there was no cover on the spur, only a few bushes and holly trees. From that angle Duncan felt they were completely exposed, and that was where the fire was coming from. Barclay was no more than five meters away, firing in a different direction. The enemy had them bracketed on three sides. Luckily they weren't getting hit from behind.

Barclay saw an insurgent across the riverbed rise up with an RPG and step out to fire. He had been behind dense vegetation, and Barclay figured he stepped forward so the foliage would not obstruct his shot. There looked to be three or four men in that fighting position supporting a PKM. Barclay shot the RPG gunner just before he could fire. The man fell back into the bushes.

"HANG!" shouted Barclay, pointing at the enemy. "HIT THAT POSITION WITH TWO-O-THREE ROUNDS!" Then Barclay turned to Gordon and yelled, "SERGEANT GORDON! DROP MORTAR ROUNDS ON THE RETREAT ROUTE BEHIND THAT ENEMY POSITION!"

Bratland saw an enemy soldier get shot and fall back into bushes across the valley. Then he heard his radio. By chance, the way he landed, the long whip on his radio was picking up a signal. Bratland could hear McKnight on the radio demanding, "ATTACK TWO-SIX; ATTACK SIX; SITREP! ATTACK TWO-SIX; ATTACK SIX; GIVE ME A SITREP!"

Bratland did not care much for his company commander. At that moment he cared for him even less. Anger arose inside him of a type he hadn't experienced since Marchetti wanted his brownie. It didn't occur to him that Attack Six had heard his initial call and then nothing else but several minutes of roaring gunfire. Attack Six undoubtedly feared the worst—that he had lost an entire squad.

Bratland had the new MOLLE vest, which enabled the strap to go over his assault pack onto his shoulder. Bratland had his hand mic-clipped on to the right shoulder strap and up to his helmet. The way he was lying it came perfectly to his face. The cord was run through that part of his shoulder so it stayed right there. It had enough slack that he could continue to talk while he shouldered his weapon and fired. He could shoot as an infantryman and do his job as a radioman at the same time.

He went to answer Attack Six several times, but the captain was still speaking into the radio, "GIVE ME A SITREP! TWO SIX; GIVE ME A SITREP!"

Finally, Bratland lost his temper.

"BREAK! BREAK! BREAK! BREAK! BREAK! ALL ATTACK ELEMENTS! THIS IS TWO-SIX ROMEO! YOU HAVE TROOPS IN CONTACT!"

SFC North's QRF: The QRF reached the vehicles, and everyone scrambled in. The turret gunners chambered their weapons, and the drivers pulled their vehicles out. They moved beyond the concertina wire that demarcated the KOP perimeter and started moving as fast as they could down the winding, *S*-turning road. North was in the lead vehicle monitoring the battle on the radio. He heard they had causalities and wondered who was hit and how badly. Two-Six Actual (Barclay) had not given a nine-line MEDEVAC yet, but the battle sounded intense so it was no wonder.

The three HMMWVs had to head north before they came to the *Y* intersect that enabled them to move south toward Landigal on the high mountain road. The QRF wasn't 200 meters out of the wire when they came under fire from enemy machineguns.

Lomen was in the second vehicle. SPC Joseph "Blue" Blake of Detroit, Michigan, was his gunner. Lomen could hear shots and see tracers. He suddenly realized they were taking fire.

"HEY!" shouted down Blake from the turret. "We're being shot at."

"SHOOT BACK!"

Blake instantly started hammering away on the .50 caliber. In the lead truck, Wilkinson drove with North in the commander's seat. Salano was in the back, and McClure was in the turret manning the M-203. McClure had never fired his weapon in combat before. He sighted in on the muzzle flashes and started pumping rounds.

"Attack Six!" called North back to Attack Main. "Attack Two-Seven! Troops in contact!"

North's HMMWV kept moving through the gunfire, and the other two HMMWVs followed until all three vehicles blew past the ambush. Then Wilkinson rounded the next spur and they broke contact.

LT Preston's Platoon; Kandigal: Rush had stopped working up a fire mission when he heard the 2nd Platoon's transmissions. It was obvious they were getting hit much

85

harder than the 1st Platoon had gotten hit because they were calling casualties. It seemed obvious to Rush that 2nd Platoon needed the assets more than he did. Then Rush heard Attack Two-Three (Lomen) report that the QRF was in contact, as well. It sounded to Rush as if 2nd Platoon had guys "breaking on the other side of despair" down near Landigal.

LT Hewerdine; O-P-Three: Hewerdine reached the ANA position farthest along the KOP's southernmost finger. His Terp Zabi was right behind him. Hewerdine was consumed by guilt and anger—guilt because Americans were under fire and he had not demanded Zman keep the ANA with the patrol, and anger, not only at the enemy for attacking the Americans, but also at the Americans for sending men into a known ambush.

Hewerdine arrived at the ANA position and told Zabi, "Tell them to get ready to move now!" Zabi did, and the ANA started scrambling up. Hewerdine took the five that were ready the fastest. Then he turned to Zabi and said, "First, tell these guys to stay with me no matter what! Second, tell Captain Zman to send reinforcements to this position till I return. Third, tell Kraus to stay put until I return." With that he turned to the five ANA and said, "LET'S GO!" and took off running down the spur heading south.

The KOP; Attack Main: Stevens, McKnight, and Dales were manning the radios. It seemed the world was exploding. The 2nd Platoon was getting hammered just a few klicks south of them. They could hear the violence of the fight over the radios, but they could also hear the roaring gunfire echoing down the valley. Aside from that, the 1st Platoon was getting hit down at Kandigal, and they just received word the QRF was also taking fire.

McKnight was wondering whether he should commit all his resources to Barclay. He knew 1st Platoon was in a firefight down at Kandigal, but he didn't know how bad their TIC was. He was waiting for Rush to follow up with coordinates for a fire mission, but McKnight was more concerned with 2nd Platoon because they had been wounded, and he could hear all the gunfire. He could hear how intense it was, and the fact that Barclay wasn't talking to him told him it was bad. McKnight had question after question, but he wasn't getting any information from his PLs.

"Do I need to get a MEDEVAC started?" he thought. "Do I need to get CAS to him? Does First Platoon need a fire mission?" He couldn't help them if they didn't give him a SITREP. "What is going on?" Just as he needed his platoon leaders to keep him informed, McKnight called his own commander at battalion headquarters in Asadabad to give him a SITREP. He picked up the hand mic on the MBITR and called battalion.

"Chosin Six! Attack Six! Chosin Six! Attack Six![xvii] We have troops in contact." Attack Main had instant messenger traffic. McKnight had Stevens on the instant messenger sending information. They would continue to send as they got it.

Stevens wondered whether the enemy was going to assault the KOP at the same time. They would never get a better chance to overrun it if they hit it in force while so many of its assets were tied up in individual fights throughout the valley.

(L-R) Eddie Hernandez, Miguel Salano, Shane Wilkinson (photo by Lomen)

2nd Platoon tent where the QRF waited (photo by Lomen)

An example of the steep, holly-bush-covered terrain (photo by Wilkinson)

An example of the rough terrain, although not steep enough to depict the spur where Barclay's patrol set up their defenses (photo by Wilkinson)

The only road into and out of the Korangal Valley (photo by Zuzzio)

The Korangal Valley Road, seen from a HMMWV (photo by Zuzzio)

"I had a pretty good idea how bad Sergeant Gean was hit. I saw his back explode. There was a lot of blood on him. Gean was firing his weapon. He had it up in the air with one arm, firing it off. A little while can be a few seconds. Everything was moving in slow motion. There was a pool of blood under him, and he was still up and firing. I don't even think he knew he was hit." Sergeant Benjamin Bleidorn, 2nd Platoon, A/1/32.

The Firefight

"ATTACK MAIN, THIS IS TWO-SIX ROMEO!" called Bratland.

"Attack Main, send it."

"ROGER," Bratland recognized Stevens's voice. "TWO-SIX ROMEO, TROOPS IN CONTACT! GRID, SAME AS LAST! PREPARE TO COPY! WE HAVE CASUALTIES!"

"Put on Two-Six Actual."

"TWO-SIX ACTUAL IS NOT AVAILABLE!"

"Where is Two-Six Actual?"

Bratland ignored the request and continued firing.

"AMMO!" shouted Duncan. "AMMO!"

Hang was lobbing 203 rounds wherever Barclay told him to. He had not taken any more fire from the village near Landigal. Hang would fire a round, then look behind him and scan their sides while he reloaded, and then fire again.

Marchetti managed to pull Gean up near the M-240B position and lay him down. He went to triage him; only, he realized he didn't have his aid bag. Somehow it had come off its lanyard. He turned and raced back to the clearing to get it.

Gordon had started the mortars popping and then called for 155 millimeters out of Blessing. The huge shells came screaming in to explode on the opposite valley wall. After Gordon had the 155s slamming, he called back to Day at the KOP and called for the second tube in a different direction. He kept the distance at 300 meters and walked the 120s in a semicircle around them. Gordon then called for a shake and bake saying, "H-E followed by Willie Pete!" switching the rounds from High Explosive to White Phosphorous. He hoped to kill the enemy, but if they weren't already on fire, he hoped to at least obscure their visibility with smoke from burning holly bushes.

Bratland saw Marchetti run in front of the M-240B. Duncan had been firing, and Marchetti unknowingly ran right into his firing lane to go back to the clearing. Bratland figured the medic had lost his mind until he saw Marchetti reach down and grab something. Was he going back for the brownie? Bratland almost laughed when he saw Marchetti grab his aid bag. He realized Doc must have forgotten it. Then Marchetti ran back to where Gean was. Duncan never stopped firing, and it seemed to Bratland a miracle that Marchetti wasn't hit.

Hang was firing 203 rounds one after another. He was hitting where Barclay told him to fire, but then he heard Gean shouting at him, "HANG! SHOOT AT THIS SPOT OVER HERE! GIVE US SOME COVERING FIRE!" Hang switched to the enemy position where Gean was pointing and started firing grenades at it.

Duncan was getting low on ammunition. He had burned through four 100 round belts and slapped in his fifth.

"AMMO!" bellowed Duncan. "I NEED AMMO!"

Yusella had no idea what was happening on the other side of the spur. All he knew was what was happening to his fire team. He knew the enemy was hitting them from across the valley, and he wanted more firepower to deal with it.

"OCOMPO!" he shouted up the spur. "OCOMPO!" Yusella quickly realized there was no way anyone above could hear him. The roaring gunfire was deafening and drowned out everything. There were explosions and ricochets along with the multiple reports and chatters of small-arms fire. He realized if he was going to get anyone's attention, he would have to send someone up to them. He looked around to see who was closest.

Caracciolo was trying to distinguish between what was a muzzle flash and what was an explosion or even a ricochet. This was only his second firefight. He continued to lob his 203 rounds where Reyna was firing. Then Yusella ran over to him.

"CROTCH! GO UP TO OCOMPO'S POSITION! I
WANT OCOMPO DOWN HERE NOW!"

Caracciolo didn't understand the order, but he wasn't going
to argue. He jumped up and ran up the hill toward Ocompo. He
could hear Quinalty's SAW firing in controlled bursts.

Gean was still firing. The recoil made it difficult to aim, so
he would fire and readjust, repeating the process. He was lying
on his side, in a second pool of blood. Marchetti jumped back
down beside him and began exposing his wound. Incoming
rounds were hammering the rocks around them. They had been
putting so much effort and firing so many rounds to kill the
wounded man that the others were amazed he was still alive.

Marchetti wanted to move him to better cover, but Gean
was too heavy. Bleidorn saw the medic struggling and ran over
to help. The two started dragging the wounded soldier up to a
better position behind a small berm. Gean looked back and saw
bullets impacting right where he had been lying.

"Oh my God!" he realized. "If Ben hadn't grabbed me right
then, I'd be dead."

Caracciolo reached Ocompo and said, "YUSELLA
WANTS YOU DOWN THERE NOW!"

If Ocompo had any problem with the order, he never
showed it. Caracciolo took his position, and Ocompo leapt up
and started down the spur toward Yusella. Caracciolo started
lobbing 203 rounds from Ocompo's position. He could clearly
see enemy muzzle flashes from a little spur on the opposite
valley. The way the spur stuck out, both Caracciolo and
Quinalty could see back down the river from where the QRF
might be arriving. They were trying to hit any enemy troops
that might ambush their QRF. He started firing grenades into
the spur. The others were all hammering away with their
weapons as well.

Marchetti and Bleidorn dragged Gean toward the berm. It
offered the only protection. Gean was dead weight and very
heavy. Bullets followed them with every step.

"HELP ME OUT!" yelled Bleidorn to his friend. He
couldn't understand why Gean wasn't using his legs. He didn't
know he was paralyzed because he thought he saw one of

Gean's legs moving, trying to help them push. They reached the berm and lay Gean down. Bleidorn immediately turned back for his position as Marchetti slapped a compress on Gean's back.

Bleidorn was running when he saw Gordon on the radio directing their fire support. Bullets were hammering around him. Gordon was squatting, directing fire, and Bleidorn noticed his friend had a bloody hole in his boot. Bleidorn ran toward Gordon and started pulling out a compress when it seemed to him he merely blinked and was somehow lying on the ground. He knew instantly he was hit because he had never felt such incapacitating pain.

"AAAGGGGHHH!" screamed Bleidorn, cupping his wounded leg. He didn't know the extent of his wound, but it was the most painful experience of his life. He had never felt such intense pain. He writhed in agony. "AAAGGHHHH! FUCK! IT HURTS! AAAGGGHHH!" His leg tried to curl behind itself. Bleidorn looked down and saw a hole in his knee. Because of the angle his leg formed while running, the bullet had gone through his patella tendon into his femur.

Rounds were still raining down all around them. Bleidorn's weapon was lying beside him. He picked it up to return fire. Only, it had fallen in the moon-dust-like dirt, causing it to malfunction. Bleidorn grabbed Gordon's M-4 and started firing again, all the while screaming in pain.

Ocompo made it down to Yusella, and the corporal told him where to fire. But then Yusella looked around for Caracciolo. "Where is Crotch?" Yusella had expected Caracciolo to come back down with Ocompo. It never occurred to him that Caracciolo would take Ocompo's position. What Yusella wanted was more firepower. All he'd managed to do was switch out a man.

Duncan could hear Barclay shouting, "WHO'S HIT? SERGEANT GEAN! WHO'S HIT?"

"GEAN IS HIT!"

"SERGEANT GORDON! CALL UP A NINE-LINE!"

"GORDON'S HIT, TOO!"

"SERGEANT BLEIDORN, WE GOT TWO GUYS DOWN!"

"I'M SHOT, TOO!"

"FUCK! HOW MANY CASUALTIES DO WE HAVE?"

Caracciolo could hear Quinalty firing, and he could tell Reyna was changing out because he heard him close the feed tray cover on his machinegun. Then he heard Reyna yell out, "AAAGGHHH!"

Caracciolo knew a cry of pain when he heard it, but he didn't know what had happened until he heard Reyna calling, "CORPORAL YUSELLA! CORPORAL YUSELLA! I'M HIT! I'M HIT!"

Caracciolo couldn't believe it. He looked at Reyna and thought, "Is he serious?" Caracciolo didn't see any blood. Reyna's head, body, and arms seemed fine. He couldn't see anything else. But then Reyna became enraged. He grabbed his SAW and held down the trigger, hammering back at the far side. He was no longer firing controlled bursts but just blazing away on full automatic.

"HEY!" shouted Yusella. "MAINTAIN FIRE DISCIPLINE! CALM DOWN!" Yusella moved over to Reyna to check on the severity of his wound. The bullet had gone through the flesh of his leg right where his boot met his calf. It was a light wound. "YOU'RE GOING TO BE OKAY! LAY DOWN SUPPRESSING FIRE!" [xviii]

Caracciolo couldn't see Marchetti, so he shouted up to let the others know Reyna was hit. He hadn't heard anything from anyone outside his fire team for the entire duration of the firefight. With all the gunfire the only voices he had heard were Yusella's, who had given him an order, and Reyna's, who had shouted in pain.

"HEY," Caracciolo shouted up, "WE NEED A MEDIC DOWN HERE!"

"HOLD ON!" responded a voice. "WE GOT CASUALTIES UP HERE!"

"Holy shit!" thought Caracciolo. He hadn't thought of the possibility that anyone else had been hit.

Bratland fired several more tracers at what appeared to be PKM muzzle flashes. Duncan pounded the site with bursts. Someone grabbed Bratland's leg and called out to him. Bratland recognized the voice. It was Gordon.

"I've been hit."

Bratland laughed. How could Gordon joke at a time like this?

"Dude, you're on the downside of the fuckin' firefight. You're on the far side of the hill. How the fuck did you get hit? You're full of shit!"

Then Bratland saw Gordon's hand was covered in blood.

"It's running over the top of my boot. Brad, I'm hit."

"Holy shit! This is fucking bad!" That was when Bratland noticed the muzzle flashes behind them on another ridge at three o'clock.

"Sergeant Gordon," called Barclay, "I need you to fire on . . ."

"I'm shot."

"Can you still do the mission?"

"Yeah, I got it."

Barclay told him where he wanted the fire, and Gordon called in the mortars. Barclay was glad he didn't have to take Gordon's job, too. He already had so much to do.

Gean lay helplessly as Marchetti rolled him onto his side to examine his wound. The gunfire was no less intense, but they were behind a small berm that provided limited cover. There were incoming and outgoing rounds flying all over the place. Explosions from RPGs erupted on their hill while 120 mortars and 155 artillery pounded the far valley. Gordon heard Marchetti calling for scissors. The medic couldn't find his. Gordon crawled over to help. He had a Combat Lifesaver Kit packed with extra bandages, scissors, and tourniquets. He handed over the scissors and looked at his friend. Gean's eyes were rolling back into his head. Gordon had no idea where or how badly Gean was hit. Gean was pale white. Gordon feared his friend was dying.

"What am I going to tell Shannon?" thought Gordon. Shannon was Gean's girlfriend. Gordon and his wife used to go out with them along with Lomen and Bleidorn and their wives.

Gean felt Marchetti cutting off his body armor. To get to it quickly, Marchetti simply cut the shoulder strap that held the body of the vest where the ceramic plates sat.

"You've lost a lot of blood," said Marchetti. Gean passed out. Gordon handed bandages from his kit to Marchetti. The medic was putting pressure on the wound to try to stem the flow of blood.

Bratland saw Gordon crawl off to a position several yards away. He was calling in fire on a separate enemy position. The enemy was hitting them from their two o'clock all the way over to their ten o'clock. Bratland returned fire at muzzle flashes several times before realizing they were outgoing 203 explosions.

Marchetti moved over to Gordon and examined his boot. Gordon brushed him off. He had to maintain the incoming artillery, and he knew the others were hit worse than him. Marchetti gave Gordon a shot of morphine for the pain.

Bratland saw Marchetti get up and run down the other side of the patrol base.

"What the hell is he doing?" thought Bratland. Then he saw Marchetti running toward them with several ammo belts. He ran up to Duncan and threw the belts down at his feet. Then he was off and running again. Bratland felt a surge of pride toward his fellow soldiers. Everyone was fighting, and Marchetti was disregarding his own life to get what the patrol needed to survive.

Barclay became aware of Stevens asking for a nine-line.

"What's the status? I need a nine-line. Start working up the nine-line."

"WAIT ONE!" said Barclay. Then he turned his head and shouted, "MARCHETTI! I NEED A NINE-LINE! GIVE ME A STATUS SO I CAN SEND IT UP!" Their medic would normally do the nine-line, but he was busy.

Marchetti started calling over battle roster numbers.

"HOW IS GEAN DOING?"

"I DON'T KNOW HOW HE'S DOING!"

"IS HE GOING TO MAKE IT?"

After a moment's hesitation Marchetti said, "Yeah. He's going to make it."

Barclay quickly wrote down the battle roster numbers and called back to Attack Main.

"THREE WOUNDED. TWO ROUTINE. ONE SERIOUS."

SFC North's QRF: The nine-lines were read off using the last four digits in a soldier's social security number followed by the foremost letter of their first and last name. Lomen heard numbers being read off followed by "C-G."

"Oh man!" he said. "I hope that's not Chase."

Then the next numbers were read. They finished with "B-B."

"No! Is that Ben?"

The next numbers followed with "A-G."

"Not Gordon, too. Oh my God!"

"Holy fuck!" thought McClure as he listened to the nine-line. "All these guys are getting hit. There can't be that many guys left over there."

Everyone in the KOP and the QRF could tell that one hell of a battle was taking place about 1,000 meters down the valley. There were tracers and explosions everywhere.

North knew his QRF would not be able to reach Barclay's patrol. The best they could do was move into a position atop the opposite valley and provide over-watch from the village of Alia Bad, enabling Barclay's soldiers to get away. They weren't halfway to Alia Bad when they took a second contact. North told Wilkinson to keep driving and called in the second contact as they blew through another ambush.

McClure was hammering back from the turret with his 203 as tracers chased the three HMMWVs along the mountain road. Behind him, in Lomen's truck, Blake was spitting tracers back at the enemy. Then they rounded a bend in the road and stopped taking fire. The column continued onward.

LT Hewerdine's ANA Ground QRF: Hewerdine reached the river bottom and started south with his five ANA in tow. He was still seething with anger. He had been moving on adrenaline and making good time. All he carried was his M-4, seven mags, and his kit. He had body armor on, but that was it, so he was able to cover ground. His ANA were even less encumbered with only their AKs and three mags apiece. They moved south down the riverbed at a fast pace.

LT Preston's Platoon; Kandigal: Rush could no longer hear enemy incoming in their area. Once they had gained fire superiority, the enemy popped smoke and faded into the valley. From that point on, Rush and Preston moved around checking on their positions and ramping up security at their O-Ps. But they were riveted to the 2nd Platoon's battle. Rush was listening to the horror that was enveloping Barclay when Attack Six came back to him.

"Do you still want that fire mission?"[xix]

"No, leave it with Second Platoon; we will fight with what we got here."

Rush had been laying off the radio. He felt the others needed all the assets and attention of Attack Main. Whatever was happening down at Landigal sounded terminal.

The KOP; Attack Main TOC: Stevens was sending the casualty information to Chosin One-One. McKnight was trying to get CAS. He already had A-10s inbound, and since they had wounded, they would need rotary wing. Blackhawks couldn't operate without an escort of two Apaches each, so they would get gun ships, too; McKnight just didn't know when. He was trying to push the assets to his men as fast as he could.

LT Barclay's Patrol: Gordon had received a shot of morphine from Marchetti and felt himself become lightheaded. He suddenly feared he might mistakenly call the wrong mission.

"Be advised," he radioed Day back at the KOP. "I've been hit. I've been given a shot of morphine. Double check my calls."

Duncan was relying completely on the others to find targets, mostly Barclay on one side and Bratland on the other. He couldn't see any muzzle flashes. Everyone was shouting that they could, but the bright emission of one's own weapon was blinding. Duncan just fired at the others' tracer strikes. He could hear guys yelling that the enemy was firing from a rock formation across the ridge. He wasn't sure where, but Bratland pointed right at it and yelled, "FIRE AT THAT ROCK FORMATION THERE!" Duncan started hitting it with bursts.

"I NEED AMMO!" shouted a voice. Bratland didn't know who it was because he could barely hear with Duncan rocking beside them with the M-240B. Bratland was almost deaf. Whoever it was grabbed his leg and shook it.

"I NEED AMMO!"

"GO INSIDE MY ASSAULT PACK!" shouted Bratland over his shoulder. "THERE ARE MAGS IN THERE!"

Bratland felt someone fishing around in his pack. Whoever it was must have found what he was looking for because after a few moments he crawled away. Then Bratland emptied a magazine and reached for a new one.

"Fuck!" he said to himself in fear. "I'm down to one mag."

Bratland initially had seven mags on his body and seven in his assault pack. He now had six empty mags, and someone had just taken from his ruck. He didn't know whether he had any more. He checked his assault pack. He had one magazine left. Bratland stopped firing. He could see muzzle flashes, but he was almost out of ammunition, and he wasn't going to waste his last rounds. It was now dark. The firefight had been raging for twenty minutes.

Platoon Sergeant North's QRF: The QRF raced to the assistance of Barclay's patrol, but in the darkness and confusion, Wilkinson missed the *Y* intersect that turned south toward Landigal. By the time he realized he had passed the turn, North was shouting at him to stop. Wilkinson slammed on

100

the brakes, and the others did, too. They were all past the turn now, in a traffic jam on a narrow road. North gave the order for the rear vehicle to reverse beyond the *Y* intersect so they could all back up. The HMMWV was doing just that when a third contact erupted.

McClure saw the vehicle was taking rounds. He tried to open fire, but all the dust that kicked up had rendered his weapon inoperable.

"SALANO!" McClure shouted down into the HMMWV. "GIVE ME YOUR WEAPON!"

McClure stuck his hand down inside the HMMWV, and Salano slapped his M-4 into it. McClure brought up the weapon with attached M-203 on it. He reached down again and was preparing to shout for a 203 round when Salano slapped the 40mm grenade in his hand. McClure brought it up, loaded the M-203, and lobbed a round at the enemy position. He couldn't see the shooters, but he could see the bright emission of their weapon in the dusk. McClure reached down again, and just like that, Salano had another 203 round in his hand.

The truck in front had stopped. They were on a big, sharp bend in the road with McClure's HMMWV on the other side. McClure couldn't see the insurgents, but he was convinced he knew exactly from where they were firing because he knew the road. Using plunging fire he wanted to lob a 203 round over the bend. Only, there was a tree right beside them that blocked him from lacing a round right on the enemy position. The truck would have to move forward or back up for him to get a shot.

Instead, McClure took careful aim and tried to lace a shell through the tree branches. It didn't work. The round hit a branch less than twenty feet from him and exploded. The force knocked McClure back down inside the truck. He felt the intense heat against his face and feared he was wounded.

"Ar-u-okay, man?" asked Salano in his thick Mexican accent. "U-okay?"

McClure got back up and continued firing 203 rounds. The enemy was over a knoll, but he couldn't see them; he could only see their flashes every time they fired on the lead truck. He could tell from the explosions that his 203 rounds were

101

landing in the vicinity of where the incoming flashes were originating, but he didn't know how close he was landing them. He marveled at how Salano had a grenade in his hand the very moment he stuck it down inside the HMMWV. The Mexican[xx] was smart and knew what to do without being told.

McClure knew it was a completely separate firefight from the Landigal firefight but expertly set up. The enemy obviously anticipated the QRF heading out because they had three separate ambushes waiting to hit them.

LT Hewerdine's ANA Ground QRF: Hewerdine estimated they were halfway to Donga. He was still mad, but his adrenaline had worn off, and he was breathing hard from the quick pace he was setting. His ANA were still right behind him. Gunfire had erupted in front of them to the south, and Hewerdine initially thought they were taking fire. Then he realized no rounds were impacting near them and the gunfire was aimed at Alia Bad or somewhere near it. He could see muzzle flashes straight ahead, firing west across the valley.

Hewerdine ordered his ANA to return fire on the flashes. He didn't know whether any of them spoke English, but they understood what he wanted when he pointed and opened fire. The Afghans blazed away with their AKs, and Hewerdine hoped it would ease the pressure on whoever was taking fire. After several unanswered bursts, he told the ANA to cease fire, and they continued forward. They were moving carefully now, expecting contact at any moment.

Hewerdine considered getting on his radio to let the mounted QRF know his small ANA QRF was in the vicinity; he didn't want them mistaking his ANA weapons for ACM weapons. However, if he called them, he feared McKnight could order a change to his mission, either to go back or to move forward.

"I'm just not ready to take his orders right now," thought Hewerdine, opting to stay off the radio.

LT Barclay's Patrol; North of Landigal: Hang watched tracers spit across the valley toward the QRF and tried to ease the pressure by launching 203 rounds into the brush from where the fire emanated. He couldn't see any muzzle flashes because of the density of the foliage, but he could see tracers come out of the brush.

Within twenty minutes of the firefight, Gordon had coms with inbound A-10s.

"CEASE FIRE!" he called back to Day. He couldn't bring the A-10s in if the mortars were firing because an errant round might accidentally hit one of the aircraft. Gordon switched back to the A-10s and tried to vector them in. However, he soon realized they had a problem. There was low cloud cover.

All the pilots could see were the tops of the mountains sticking out of the dense clouds. Gordon had his Ground Commander's Pointer (GCP), which was like a high-powered infrared laser, but he couldn't get it through the clouds to show the A-10s where they were. Normally, Gordon only had to point it in the air, and it was like a beacon in the night, but tonight it wasn't visible because of the density of the clouds.

"We can see Asadabad," said one of the pilots, trying to vector in using landmarks.

"You are nowhere near me if you can see Asadabad."

Gordon couldn't get them in. The A-10s were flying in a wagon wheel from Abbas Ghar Mountain to Asadabad because of the cloud cover. They could not come down to engage.

The A-10s were doing the right thing by procedures, but Bratland didn't know that. To him it was simply nighttime, and he had no idea there was cloud cover. Bratland could hear everything over his radio and thought the pilots were afraid to engage. He could hear some of what the pilot was saying, something about not being sure of where they were in relation to the enemy. The A-10s weren't going to unload and maybe kill some friendlies. However, at that point, Bratland knew they were getting shot at and shot up and were scarcely low on ammo. Bratland almost shouted into the radio, "We are fuckin' black on everything! We need suppressing fire now!"

Gordon was very frustrated. He continued to give the A-10s his grid, but they kept talking about being able to see A-bad. They had the strobes and he continually marked their position with GCP. In desperation he even repeated their grid, knowing he was not supposed to do that. He didn't know what else to do. None of their marking techniques were working.

"Come in on this heading," he said, trying to guide them in, "and drop below the cloud cover." He knew if he could just bring them into the valley, once below the clouds they would have plenty of room to move. However, the pilots weren't going to risk their lives or their aircraft on a soldier they didn't know. They did not come down.

In frustration, Gordon gave up on the circling A-10s and switched over to the mortar net to talk to Day.

"Listen, I can't do anything with these guys. They are fuckin' useless. Get them out of there and get the Apaches in here. As soon as the A-tens are out, start with H-E on the last T-R-P." They hadn't been able to use the mortars with the A-10s circling overheard. Since Gordon couldn't have the air support, he wanted the mortars and hoped he'd have more luck when the Apaches arrived.

Bratland saw Barclay moving and knew, as the LT's RTO, that he should be following him. He raced after Barclay.

The lieutenant was trying to get an assessment and find out exactly how many of his men were wounded and who they were. He was forced to move back up the hill where there was more cover because directly to his front was open terrain. But every time he moved, he drew fire and was forced to take the prone position. He couldn't understand how the enemy could spot him so easily in the dense brush. Then he saw Bratland dive down beside him, his long whip radio extending high into the air. Barclay instantly realized why the bullets were following him.

"GET THAT DAMN LONG WHIP DOWN! YOU'RE GOING TO GET ME SHOT!" Barclay kept moving. He worked his way around their perimeter trying to get a feel for their situation.

Caracciolo saw Barclay move down to Reyna's position. Caracciolo didn't stop to watch; he was busy fighting and put another 203 round at a muzzle flash across the valley.

The firefight was raging when Barclay found Reyna in a state of shock. The specialist was having a hard time keeping his composure. Barclay got right down in Reyna's face and looked him in the eye.

"Hey!" he said forcefully. "We need you! We've got guys hurt a lot worse than you! You need to suck it up and continue to fight!"

"Okay," said Reyna, pulling himself together. "I got it."

Barclay turned and went back up the hill. Caracciolo didn't hear what was said, but he saw Barclay move back to where he had come from. But for the sound of everyone's weapons, Caracciolo thought his fire team was alone on the mountain.

Barclay had completed a check of their perimeter and found they only had four wounded. Gean and Bleidorn were up to Barclay's right. Reyna was down to his left, and Gordon was back in the trees where he was heading. He got back and slid down behind cover as Gordon said, "We've got two Apaches inbound, two minutes out."

BATTLE STORYBOARD

KOP

1-32

LEDGEND

Last KOP ANA Posit
Mounted QRF Route ————
Ground QRF (ETT and ANA)
ETT and ANA Exfill route

***View From KOP OP1

Basic Situation: US and ANA (ETT) forces sent two patrols out to conduct presents patrols in local villages in order to deny the enemy access to the villages for resupply or anti government activities.

1LT Barkley's patrol was engaged, sustained

Battle storyboard (1) by LT Hewerdine

BATTLE STORYBOARD

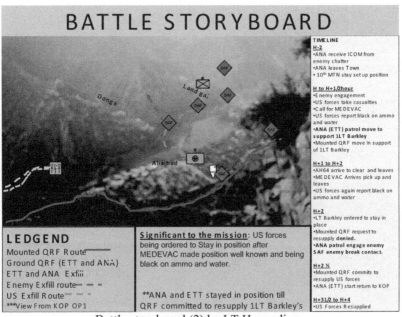

Donga

Landga

Alia bad

TIMELINE

H-2
•ANA receive ICOM from enemy chatter
•ANA leaves Town
• 10th MTN stay set up position

H to H+1/2hour
•Enemy engagement
•US forces take casualties
•Call for MEDEVAC
•US forces report black on ammo and water
•ANA (ETT) patrol move to support 1LT Barkley
•Mounted QRF move in support of 1LT Barkley

H+1 to H+2
•AH64 arrive to clear and leaves
•MEDEVAC Arrives pick up and leaves
•US forces again report black on ammo and water

H+2
•LT Barkley ordered to stay in place
•Mounted QRF request to resupply **denied.**
•ANA patrol engage enemy **SAF enemy break contact.**

H+2 ½
•Mounted QRF commits to resupply US forces
•ANA (ETT) start return to KOP

H+31/2 to H+4
•US Forces Resupplied

LEDGEND

Mounted QRF Route
Ground QRF (ETT and ANA)
ETT and ANA Exfill
Enemy Exfill route — — —
US Exfill Route — —
***View From KOP OP1

Significant to the mission: US forces being ordered to Stay in position after MEDEVAC made position well known and being black on ammo and water.

**ANA and ETT stayed in position till QRF committed to resupply 1LT Barkley's

Battle storyboard (2) by LT Hewerdine

106

"There were rounds going everywhere. They had us dialed in perfect. There was a ton of them. There was a shit ton, that's all I know. I remember thinking, 'There's no way I'm going to survive this.' I'd never seen that many muzzle flashes in my life. It took four Apaches to clear them out. They did a gun-run and unloaded all their two-point-seven-five rockets. You know the little pod they have of eight on each side? They are pretty big explosion, lit up the whole canyon. There was a couple seconds there it was like broad daylight. It was beautiful. They were treetop low. I remember when one launched all those rockets, he was right above us, maybe thirty or forty feet above the trees. I about pissed myself because I thought he was firing at us, because of how low he was. Those two birds launched, and after they fired themselves black, they took off. Then the next two came in."
Specialist Nick Bratland, 2nd Platoon RTO, A/1/32.

Apaches on Station

Preston and Rush could hear Attack Six and Attack Two-Six conversing on the company net. They could also hear the heavy *whumps* of 120 mortars and the louder *booms* of 155s echoing down the valley. Then the 1st Platoon heard the unmistakable sound of helicopters roaring in along the Pesch. Their thunder grew louder and louder. Two Apaches came flying across the Pesch into the Korangal passing almost right over Kandigal on their way into the valley. Right behind them was a Blackhawk. At almost that same time, Rush took a call saying they had predator coverage.

LT Barclay's Patrol: Barclay and Gordon were on their radios; Bratland was listening on his. Barclay sent the initial nine-line to Attack Main, and then Gordon sent one. Barclay sent the updated nine-line that included Reyna's number. Meanwhile, Gordon was talking to the inbound Apaches. He switched to Blessing to call off the 155s and then to the KOP to let Day know to be ready to stand down with their 120s. Finally he made coms with the Blackhawks for MEDEVAC. Barclay was talking to Attack Six and giving them the locations of known enemy positions.

LT Hewerdine's ANA QRF; North of Donga:
"GET DOWN!" bellowed Hewerdine to his ANA soldiers.
"GET INTO THE BRUSH! FUCKIN' STAY DOWN!"

Hewerdine dove for cover. He could hear the Apaches roaring up the valley. He prayed the choppers would not mistake them for the enemy. All they had to mark themselves as friendly were the IR strips on their uniforms, not always easily seen through night vision.

"This is stupid!" Hewerdine said to himself. "I let my emotions drag me into a fuckin' bad spot!" Hewerdine looked up and saw the AH-64s pass almost directly overheard. They were moving fast, heading south down the valley, ominous and terrifying. Again he thought, "This is stupid. What the hell am I doing out here? I'm going to get myself killed."

Hewerdine once more thought of radioing back to inform Attack Main of his position. However, he still did not like the idea of possibly being ordered to do something by McKnight that he thought was tactically unsound. He still had control of his small element and he wanted to keep it that way. He decided just to sit tight and listen.

Attack Main TOC: McKnight was trying to take in all the information and come up with the best course of action. He was frustrated the A-10s had been unable to provide support. In fact, they had actually drawn support off the beleaguered patrol because they had called off the indirect mortars and 155s to allow the aircraft to come in. He was glad the Apaches were arriving but worried they were too late. Then he received a call from them.

"Hey, I got six guys in the stream bed," said the pilot. He gave grid coordinates and requested permission to open fire.

"No," said McKnight, perplexed, "that is not where the enemy is."

"Well, I got six guys who definitely have weapons. Do I have permission to fire?"

"No, I don't know who that is. Don't shoot those guys."[xxi]

108

LT Barclay's Patrol; North of Landigal: By now everyone could hear the Apaches. They came right up the valley, the sound of their rotors getting progressively ominous. They came rolling in and Gordon switched back to them. Gordon continued with the mortars and artillery but almost salivated at the thought of air support arriving, as that was his specialty.

In fact, Gordon had even gotten in trouble with the battalion FSNCO because he had spent as much time teaching his men how to use Apaches and A-10s as he had their indirect mortars and artillery. Gordon simply did not understand that kind of thinking. In Iraq he had gotten used to using air support instead of mortars and artillery because they caused far less collateral damage. In Iraq they hadn't been allowed to use artillery because they ended up blowing city blocks to pieces. But Apaches were different. They could come in and give pinpoint air support without damaging anything but the bad guys.

"Prepare to engage as soon as you come up the valley," advised Gordon.

SFC North's QRF; Just South of Alia Bad: McClure became aware of the sound of helicopters over the din of the firefight. Once the enemy heard the helicopters, they broke and ran. The QRF took no more incoming fire once the Apaches could be heard. The QRF drove down the road to the south until they were in position to provide over-watch. They were almost directly across from Donga.

North could see Barclay's strobes across the valley and figured the Apaches and Blackhawks would have no trouble locating him. Tracers were still knifing back and forth in the darkness, but everyone on the QRF knew that was going to change very soon. The Apaches had thermal imaging. They could see in the dark.

Jalalabad; Chosin One-One TOC: Major Paul Garcia and the 1st Battalion staff were trying to get as many assets to Attack Company's beleaguered patrol as was possible. Garcia was back and forth on the radio from Attack Main to the Asadabad air assets which included A-10s, Apaches, and MEDEVAC Blackhawks. It was another bad night.

With only one US infantry brigade in all of Afghanistan supported by only one air brigade, each battalion was spread thinly throughout the entire country, as was the CAS.

The 1st Battalion, Chosin One-One, had an AO of four valleys: the Korangal, the Waygol, the Shiriak, and the Pesch. It was a nightmare for Garcia, the battalion S-2, to try to get the meager air assets they had to support and supply their three companies, which were spread so thinly over such large areas of terrain. The whole operational construct was at a constant level of risk. Just the way the battalion was forced to array its troops made for a near-impossible situation. Captain Dug Sloan had Bravo Company in the Waygol and Shiriak Valley. Stanton had the Pesch. McKnight had the Korangal, with Captain Joe Evans's two Delta platoons from the battalion motorized company and an MP platoon to clear out the roads along the Pesch that led to all three. Garcia knew nobody had an easy mission.

Only two weeks before, they had a similar situation at Shadugay, just up from Combat Company in the Pesch. On 24 July an element under Stanton's command had been in a similar situation that resulted in one KIA. That had been very frustrating, as the enemy had gotten away. Now, McKnight's Attack Company was in a similar situation. Garcia was trying to get all the assets he could to them. They did not want the enemy to get away again.

LT Barclay's Patrol; North of Landigal: Among Barclay, Gordon, and Bratland, they had redundant coms. Since they were each fighting their own separate battle, they didn't always hear each other. In fact, Barclay wasn't aware Bratland had even been on the net. Bratland, for his part, mostly listened but didn't wait to be told to get on the radio if he thought it needed to be done. He could hear the birds getting close. Unlike the A-10s, the Apaches were below the cloud cover.

110

"ANY AIRCRAFT IN THE AREA!" he still had to shout to be heard over the gunfire. "TROOPS IN CONTACT! READY AIR SUPPORT REQUESTED!" He then gave their grid coordinates. One of the Apache pilots responded. He said he wanted them to better mark their perimeter so he knew exactly where the friendlies were.

"WE'VE GOT FOUR STROBES MARKING OUR PERIMETER!"

The pilot confirmed he saw the strobes but asked for additional clarification using a Ground Commander's Pointer. Bratland didn't have a GCP. Barclay did, but he wasn't beside him. Barclay was on the radio himself, using his GCP to mark enemy positions. But the Apache pilot was asking for someone to mark their friendly perimeter.

Bratland thought to himself, "This guy wants a fucking neon sign saying, 'Friendlies right here!'" Although they weren't four nice, neat corners, Bratland couldn't understand why the pilot needed further demarcation. If he just connected those four strobes, he'd have their entire perimeter. The Apache pilot asked Bratland to take a GCP and make a circle above their perimeter. The GCP was very bright and could be seen from miles away. However, at that point, other than the four strobes, which Bratland couldn't see, he had no idea where their perimeter was. He didn't know who else had been shot, who hadn't been shot, who'd been moved, or whether they had collapsed down on their perimeter.

Then Bratland felt someone tug on him. He looked down and saw Gordon beside him. Gordon was on his own radio, guiding in the helicopters. He had been trying to signal with the GCP, but the holly bush was too tall. Gordon was sitting because of his gunshot wound. He had trouble standing. He handed Bratland his M-4 with mounted GCP.

"Do it," said Gordon, "just fuckin' do it. He needs you to make a circle; I'm betting he needs a circle." Gordon would have stood up to do it himself, but he couldn't put any weight on his leg, and it was hell just trying to get his six-foot-six-inch body up on one leg with all his gear still on him.

111

"Damn," thought Bratland, "that's a good forward observer, knows exactly what is needed."

Bratland grabbed Gordon's M-4 and made the circle. Barclay was still marking the enemy position with his own GCP. No sooner had Bratland marked their position than the pilot circled back to confirm. Bratland flashed again. What happened next would encourage any friendly soldier and strike fear into the enemy. To Gordon, it was awesome.

The Apaches thundered up the valley just blasting away with their chain guns and 2.75-inch rockets. They had thermo-imaging and used it to deadly effect.

Barclay thought he knew where the main enemy cells were. They had been hit from all over three sides, but they had three concentrated positions. Barclay had his GCP aimed right at one of them.

Gordon called back to the KOP and ordered, "CEASE FIRE!" to stop the mortars. He didn't want an errant 120 round to inadvertently hit one of the Apaches. Then he retrieved his M-4 from Bratland and fought his way to a standing position. He stood on one leg and aimed his own GCP at another enemy location. Barclay and Gordon orchestrated, while the others simply watched the explosions. The Apaches swooped in on an attack run. The first Apache came in on Barclay's target, and just as it finished, the second Apache came in while the first moved on to Gordon's.

Gordon knew the enemy never left their dead. He figured they were retrieving them or at least tending any casualties. If so, he wanted them annihilated. Gordon knew which direction the KOP was, so he gave the Apaches an attack heading that wagon wheeled them in a direction away from the incoming mortars. The very moment the Apaches finished their run, he was back on the radio.

"FIRE!" he called to the mortars. Gordon kept them firing right up until the Apaches made their next gun run. Barclay laid his GCP on an enemy position from where they had just taken fire, and the helicopters came back around for a second run.

"CEASE FIRE!" Gordon called to Day.

Instantly the 120s stopped. The first Apache came back in with rockets and chain guns blazing. Once it passed Barclay's marking, it moved on to Gordon's again while the second swooped in on Barclay's. The moment the helicopters made their runs and passed out of the loop, Gordon called back to Day.

"FIRE!"

The mortars started up again. Gordon walked the rounds right behind the position where he last saw machinegun fire and kept them there until the Apaches came around for a third run.

"CEASE FIRE!" shouted Gordon.

The first Apache again swooped in on Barclay's GCP marking, hammering away. If anyone was over there, they were dead or severely wounded. Then the bird passed to Gordon's and did the same while the second hit Barclay's again. The moment they were clear, Gordon shouted, "FIRE!"

Anything outside their IR strobes got nailed by the Apaches. Bratland felt they had to have hit somebody because wherever they fired, the gunfire stopped. By now everyone had their night vision on. They could see the Apaches flying almost directly overhead. Usually they were 200 to 300 meters away, but sometimes they came to within 100 meters.

Gordon then got word they had two more Apaches inbound, already in the Korangal Valley, two minutes out. That was good because the first two birds were shooting themselves black. The Apaches were escorting the MEDEVAC. Since there were two Blackhawks total, and each Blackhawk had to have two Apaches as escort, they had four Apaches. The first two Apaches fired themselves black and wheeled off.

Barclay knew they needed to get a casualty collection point (CCP) prepared so they could evacuate their wounded. He told Marchetti and the others to find a spot suitable for the Blackhawks to at least drop a jungle extractor. He knew there was no way any bird could land. The KOP was the only flat piece of ground in the entire region. That was why they put Attack Main there.

Duncan called out to Hang and Ocompo to make sure they were okay. They were. The major portion of the firing was over, although they were still taking occasional rounds.

LT Hewerdine's ANA QRF; North of Donga:
Hewerdine and his five ANA soldiers had been hugging the ground since the Apaches first flew over. Hewerdine was worried they might mistake his small patrol for insurgents. While the first Apaches were lighting up the canyon ahead, he considered trying to get out of there, but he decided against movement of any kind. Just when Hewerdine was again wondering whether they should move, he heard the sound of more helicopters coming. He and the ANA tried to melt into the ground.

LT Barclay's Patrol; North of Landigal: Caracciolo heard someone yell down that they needed an extra man to help carry wounded to the CCP.

"I'll do it." He climbed up and was told to go over and help move Bleidorn. The first thing Caracciolo saw was Gean, using his arms to low-crawl.

"Is he hurt?" thought Caracciolo. "No, he's just using his arms to crawl. He's fine." Caracciolo had no idea Gean had been wounded and couldn't understand why he was crawling. But Gean was his squad leader. Caracciolo wasn't going to question what his squad leader did.

It was suddenly very quiet. Caracciolo could barely even hear the helicopters. He could hear the others talking and getting casualties taken care of. Caracciolo moved over and stooped next to Bleidorn. They had to move all the wounded down to a lower position that jutted out, so the Blackhawks could lower a basket without slamming into the side of the mountain.

Marchetti turned to Caracciolo and said, "Crotch, Sergeant Gean's wounded. Go sit with Gean." The light bulb went off in Caracciolo's head, and he realized why Gean had been crawling. He moved over, and just as he sat down beside him, they heard the next two Apaches coming.

"Here they come, Sergeant Gean," he said. The second pair of Apaches flew right over them and began hammering away with their 30mm machineguns. Caracciolo could hear the shell casings falling, clinking off nearby rocks on the side of the valley wall.

Bratland heard the second two Apaches identify themselves as Fullback 2-4 and Fullback 4-5. When the second pair of Apaches came in, they were treetop low. They came right over the patrol's position, maybe thirty or forty feet off the spur. They began launching their rockets, and Bratland almost urinated in terror because he thought they accidentally misidentified them and were firing on Barclay's men. Then he watched the rockets soar across the valley and slam into the opposite side. Their explosions were huge and lit up the whole canyon. There were a couple seconds where it appeared to Bratland to be broad daylight. Bratland didn't see the birds taking any fire, and it surprised him.

Gean did not feel well. He knew he had lost a lot of blood, and he reasoned that was why he was having so much trouble thinking. He knew all his soldiers had been through Combat Life Saver courses and knew how to give IVs. They'd all learned basic battlefield medical treatment.

"Crotch," said Gean in almost a mumble. "Stick me with an I-V." Caracciolo was preparing to do it, but he got nervous. He always had trouble with IV sticks in CLS class.

"I'll do it," said Marchetti. He made the stick while Caracciolo held the bag, and Gean instantly felt better. His mind cleared, and he was able to think. Gean breathed and lit up a cigarette. He didn't worry about a glow signature in the darkness. He didn't care whether a sniper shot him. He became aware of Bleidorn sitting beside him, also smoking. Gean had been given morphine, and his pain was tolerable.

Bleidorn had also been given morphine, but for some reason it wasn't working on him. Bleidorn was in great pain. It was all he could do to keep from crying out while he smoked. It was some consolation to the two gunshot soldiers that they could sit and watch the Apaches make their runs firing their hellfires and 30mm guns. They hoped the copters were killing

115

all the insurgents. It looked as though they were. The Apaches were just lighting up the opposite sides of the valley.

While the Apaches swept the mountainsides for signs of the enemy, Barclay's soldiers searched for an LZ. The only thing they could find was a little spot on the side of the ridgeline where it was big enough to lay the wounded down.

Meanwhile, Attack Six was trying to control the Apaches from Attack Main. Barclay had relayed the known enemy positions, but he hadn't come on the radio in almost five minutes. Barclay had been getting a CCP up, checking his perimeter, and getting coms with the Blackhawks. Once he had that taken care of, he got back on the radio.

"I GOT IT!" he told Attack Six. "COMMANDER ON THE GROUND!" He continued aiming his GCP and told the Apaches where to go.

Quinalty was waiting for the enemy to try to come in behind them or start a fresh assault. It was now so dark that even with his night vision, it was hard to see anything. Suddenly Quinalty became aware of Gordon beside him. The tall FSO was on the radio talking to someone, and Quinalty didn't know whether it was Attack Main or the incoming Blackhawks, but the conversation was about the upcoming MEDEVAC. Quinalty thought Gordon was so intent on what he was doing that he didn't seem even to be aware of him, which, of course, he had to have been as Gordon put his elbow on Quinalty's shoulder to help support him. It was still very loud, and Quinalty couldn't hear the full extent of what was being said, but he heard Gordon say, "My foot is bleeding. My boot is full of blood."

Gordon was so tall that even bent over and favoring one leg, he towered over the heavier-built but shorter Quinalty. They were on a flat point where it leveled off, the only spot where the helicopters could hope to put a rope down to them without hitting the side of the mountain. Quinalty could tell Gordon had been given morphine because he was in a relaxed state, but he was still doing his job and doing it well. Gordon had always been good at his job—a position above his rank Quinalty felt he did better than most officers

To Quinalty, Gordon was an interesting personality. Quinalty considered himself to be raised in a middle-class family, but he considered Gordon to be one class above him when it came to upbringing. Gordon always did the right thing and he got whatever needed to be done done. Quinalty thought Gordon was an extremely competent soldier.

The Apaches stayed on station. The pilots used their thermals to sweep the valley and scan for the enemy. Barclay was in coms with them when they called back and said, "You are not in any danger. You are clear to bring MEDEVAC and get your guys out."

When the Blackhawks arrived, Quinalty helped Gordon hop on his one leg over to the CCP. He noticed Gordon could not put any weight on his gunshot foot. Gordon hadn't looked at his foot and decided he wouldn't until after everything calmed down. Marchetti tried to, but Gordon told him to take care of Gean and Bleidorn. Gordon knew Bleidorn and especially Gean were hurt a lot worse than he was.

"AAAAGGGHHHH," groaned Bleidorn, trying to fight the pain. "FUCK IT HURTS!"

Marchetti handed Caracciolo gauze and said, "Find the spot where the blood is. Put it there and wrap it up."

Caracciolo wrapped it, but he wrapped it too tightly.

"AAAGGGHHHH!" yelled Bleidorn.

"Sorry, Sergeant," said Caracciolo as he loosened it. Then he re-wrapped it.

"Crotch," asked Bleidorn in fear, "did it hit the femoral?"

"No," said Caracciolo, "doesn't look like it."

Caracciolo put his assault pack under Bleidorn's leg. Bleidorn and Gean were lying there. Marchetti whispered to Caracciolo, "Check him. Talk to him. Keep him calm."

"Hey, everything's going to be fine," said Caracciolo. "We got MEDEVAC on the way. The Q-R-F is over there providing security force. You're getting out of here."

Caracciolo saw that Gean's IV bag was empty. He called over to Marchetti, "Hey, Doc, this bag is almost empty. Do you want me to switch it out?"

"Yeah. No, I'll do it."

SFC North's QRF; South Side of Alia Bad: The first Blackhawk saw the QRF's strobes and thought they were Barclay's patrol. They flew in and hovered over the QRF. North stood waving them off and called to Barclay on the MBITR to flash his GCP. All the QRF were wearing their night vision. North could see the strobes marking Barclay's position. Then he saw the strong beam of light as Barclay flashed his GCP. The Blackhawk wheeled around and headed south-southeast toward Barclay's position.

North was worried about his soldiers and called back to Barclay asking, "Hey, how they holding up? How is it going?"

"They're alive," said Barclay. "Gean's messed up pretty bad."

The KOP; Attack Main TOC: McKnight continued to keep battalion abreast of the situation when he got a call from his BC. His commander was very unhappy.

"They were supposed to be ambushing the enemy, and they got ambushed?" said the BC in frustration. McKnight didn't know what to say. They had been trying to use guerrilla tactics against the insurgents. It obviously didn't work. Their enemy was from the Korangal. They knew the valleys like the back of their hands.[xxii] There was no use talking about what should have happened. McKnight told his commander the facts of the situation and got back to coordinating his company's efforts. He still had 1st Platoon at Kandigal, the QRF at Darbart, and Barclay's men between Landigal and Donga to consider.

"Well," said the BC, "we just got shot up. How are we going to put pressure back on the enemy?" The BC was very concerned for McKnight put pressure on the enemy.

"We can continue the mission to Landigal," said McKnight.

"Okay, let's do that."

LT Barclay's Patrol; North of Landigal: Bratland helped Caracciolo get Bleidorn into position to be airlifted. Only, he kept bumping the wounded sergeant's knee. Bleidorn would involuntarily scream. Barclay could tell the others were

118

having a difficult time moving Bleidorn because he was such a big soldier. Barclay was just moving down to help when someone accidentally grabbed the sergeant's gunshot knee causing Bleidorn to bellow, "YOU FUCKIN' RETARD! THAT'S THE LEG THAT GOT SHOT!"

Quinalty helped Marchetti and Yusella pick up Gean to carry him to the LZ. Gean was delirious from the morphine and kept repeating, "Q, take care of me. Q, you better not drop me." He was passing in and out of consciousness. Marchetti, Quinalty, and Yusella carried Gean over to where they were going to lift him with the jungle extractor, but the long day and violent firefight had sapped their strength. Gean was heavy, and Marchetti was exhausted. Caracciolo took over for the exhausted medic and helped carry his gunshot squad leader.

"I can't feel my legs," said Gean fearfully, looking up at Caracciolo. Gean's lower back was in agony. Even as drugged up as he was, the pain kept him conscious. Every little bit of movement was a stab to the nerves in his lower back.

"It's the morphine," said Caracciolo. He had no idea how badly Gean was hit and was just doing what Marchetti told him to do. "Everything's going to be fine. You're getting out of here."

Everyone was so tired that it was difficult to carry the wounded. Gean was heavy, and Bleidorn was even heavier. Caracciolo didn't know who, but someone took over for him so he went back up the hill. Caracciolo then went over and helped Reyna.

"Put your arm around me and use me as a crutch." Reyna did, and Caracciolo helped him down.

Bratland watched the Blackhawk drop a cord down; it reminded him of an anchor. A flight medic dropped down first. He prepped the wounded for airlift.

"DON'T MOVE ME!" screamed Bleidorn in agony. "DON'T MOVE ME!" Then, trying to gain composure, he winced, "Please, please put me down. It hurts too much."

They stopped, and then Bleidorn realized he had to get to the LZ area. "Don't listen to me," he said. "Just keep dragging

119

me. When I tell you to stop, ignore me. It just hurts so damn bad!"

They began dragging Bleidorn again, and even though they tried to protect his shattered leg and keep it from moving, it would move. The pain was unbearable.

"AAAAGGGGHHHH FUUUUUCK!"

"Damn, Sarge, sorry," said Bratland. "We're trying to get you outta here. Sorry about hittin' your knee."

"DON'T WORRY ABOUT HITTING MY KNEE, JUST BE FUCKIN' QUIET!" bellowed Bleidorn. "I'M IN A LOT OF FUCKIN' PAIN, AND I'M AGITATED! SHUT THE FUCK UP AND BE QUIET AND GET THIS SHIT DONE!" Bratland could tell Bleidorn just wanted everything to be over.

Bratland could tell Gean was in similar pain. It was the strangest moment of Bratland's life, when they were strapping Gean down into the litter to lift him off. It was the expression on Gean's face. It seemed to Bratland Gean had stopped caring.

They received reports from the Blackhawk that they had enemy moving down the ridgeline above them—the only place during the fight from which they had not been attacked. Hang was ordered to launch several 203 rounds upwards to clear out the ridgeline. Why the helicopters didn't engage, no one understood.

Then the Blackhawk pilot called down and told Barclay their strobes were interfering with the Blackhawk's night vision. Bratland could hear the pilots over his ASIP.

"TWO-SIX! TWO-SIX! You need to turn your strobes off! They are interfering with our night vision! You need to turn your strobes off! We know where you are!"

"TURN THE STROBES OFF!" shouted Barclay. With all his sergeants gone, Barclay passed word to Yusella, a corporal and the highest ranking man Barclay had left, to have one of his soldiers go get them.

"CROTCH!" called out Yusella. "GO BACK UP AND GRAB THE STROBE! YOU NEED TO TURN IT OFF! THE BLACKHAWK HAS NIGHT VISION AND THE STROBE IS MESSING IT UP!"

Since the air assets already had the patrol's position, they didn't need the strobes to mark their perimeter. Caracciolo climbed back up and went to grab it, but the wind from the helicopter was so strong that it blew the strobes forward and down the side of the mountain. Instead of letting it go, Caracciolo jumped down after it. He lost his footing and slid down the deep embankment. He was able to grab it, but with all the wind and dust and debris, it was hard to get back up. He decided he would stay put until the birds left. It was almost impossible to climb with all that debris swirling around.

In testament to the force generated by the hovering Blackhawk's rotors, Marchetti's aid bag was blown off the side of the mountain. The intense gusts of wind kicked up by the Blackhawk sent the bag flying off the side of the spur. The exasperated, exhausted medic had to go down after it.

"You still have one strobe on!" Bratland heard the Blackhawk pilot say. The helicopter was almost on top of them, right over the LZ. "You need to turn it off!"

The fourth one they couldn't locate. Bratland started off down below the Landing Zone. He was already near it from carrying Bleidorn down. Bratland found the strobe using his night vision and simply covered it with his body, burying it in his stomach. He was facing the LZ so he could see the Blackhawk lower its jungle extractor, but rocks and sticks were flying around like little missiles, slamming into his helmet and face.

"Thank God I put the clear lens in my Oakleys," thought Bratland to himself as rocks and sticks flew into his face. Everyone was issued Oakley ballistic sunglasses. They were extremely durable—so much so that when an IED went off, wounding Bratland in Khogiyani two months before, the glasses had saved Bratland's eyes. They were intact but lodged with steel fragments.

Bratland had the strobe buried beneath his knees and stomach, and he tried to worm backwards away from the rotor wash, but it didn't work. He backed into a tree stump. He lay there listening to the radio.

They put Gean in a skidco and hoisted him up first because he was the worst off. Immediately the cage-like stretcher started spinning. Bleidorn looked up and saw the basket whirling in a circle like the helicopter blades as Gean was winched up. By the time Gean reached the top, he was dizzy and nauseated. The Crew Chief pulled him into the Blackhawk, and Gean promptly threw up over everything.

Then they lowered the basket for Bleidorn. Bratland heard the Blackhawk pilot over his ASIP say, "You need to turn that strobe off. It's dimmed, but it's still interfering with our night vision. You need to turn it off."

Bratland could see the lights of the bird through his own night vision. There was so much rock and debris that his glasses were blown off. He covered both his eyes with his hands and wormed around until he could get one hand down to fiddle with the strobe. He finally got the strobe turned off. Then through slits in his fingers, he looked up and saw how close the Blackhawk was.

"God," he thought, "I could reach up and touch it."

Then they hooked Bleidorn up to the skidco. The flight medic strapped him in and gave the signal to pull him up. The winch kicked in, and he began to go up when the skidco collapsed on itself.

"AAAAAGGGGGHHHHH!" screamed Bleidorn as his broken leg was bent up into his face. He was spinning uncontrollably, dangling from a helicopter over the side of the spur. He had never felt such agony—not even ten minutes before when he thought it couldn't get any worse.

"AAAAAGGGGGHHHHH!"

Screaming the entire time, Bleidorn was winched up and pulled in by the Crew Chief. Gean knew his friend well and had never known him to show any inconvenience when it came to pain. Gean saw the Crew Chief straddle Bleidorn. He was trying to strap him in so they could get out of there, but the pain Bleidorn felt was almost unbearable. He couldn't stop screaming.

Gean could hear his friend's agony over the roar of the helicopter engines, and it enraged him.

122

"THE MORPHINE'S NOT WORKING ON HIM! GET THE FUCK OFF HIM!" The crew chief was obviously terrified they were going to take a rocket and was trying to secure them so they could get out of there before they got shot down. He was hurrying as fast as he could as Bleidorn screamed. Gean kept shouting, "GET OFF HIM! GET THE FUCK OFF HIM!"

He got Bleidorn secured and rolled off him onto one knee shouting, "GO! GO!" The pilot wheeled around and hit the throttle. The Blackhawk picked up speed and started racing north.

Once the first Blackhawk moved off, the second one came in. Barclay had a difficult time getting his soldiers to stay focused on the enemy and to pull security. Everyone was concerned about the wounded and trying to help. Gean, Bleidorn, and Gordon were not only their friends, but also their sergeants. They were used to telling the others what to do. Now they were all wounded. Barclay told Duncan and Yusella to keep their men alert and watching for the enemy. He had their Terp help gather up the IBA and other items removed from the wounded.

Barclay did not like having any of his men, himself included, below the hovering helicopter. At any moment he feared an RPG would come screaming in and slam into the defenseless bird. If that happened, everyone below it would probably die.

Gordon took all his ammo out and handed it over to the others. He knew they were going to need all they could get. Then he handed over his M-4, and all his sensitive equipment, radios, and batteries. He hated the idea of leaving the others.

"You get on the bird first, Sergeant," said Reyna. "You're hurt worse than I am." Reyna had a flesh wound to the leg, but he could at least put pressure on his foot. Gordon could not stand or move his foot without excruciating pain. Nevertheless, Gordon was the acting FSO and an NCO. There was no way he was going to go first.

"No, you go."

Reyna was hoisted up and taken aboard. Then it was Gordon's turn. He looked around at the others and feared he would never see them again. It was unthinkable that they would be moving alone in that area without an FO. He didn't want to leave, but he knew he was combat-ineffective and couldn't move. He didn't want them walking back because they had been understrength at the outset. Now they had just lost four men and were black on ammo. And they would have to lug the equipment and body armor of the wounded.

But Gordon knew he didn't have an option. He had to go. He was still connected to Day at the KOP. He put the phone to his mouth and said, "Tell Key [Corey Key] not to get too comfortable because I'll be back for my job." Then he handed his radio over to Marchetti and was helped to the extractor. He was tied on and hoisted up. Once he was aboard the Blackhawk, the flight medic was winched up, and then the pilot turned and headed back down the valley.

The soldiers on the ground listened as the helicopters got farther and farther away. Caracciolo crawled back up to join the others, as did Marchetti, who had been unable to find his aid bag. Then the sound of the helicopter rotors disappeared altogether, and there was nothing but absolute silence. It seemed strange to everyone present. For the last two hours they had heard nothing but machinegun fire and explosions or roaring engines. Now there was nothing—not even the sound of insects or wind through the trees. The night air was deathly still.

"The walk back felt really hopeless. It was the first time in my life where I didn't know what was going to come next, and I can't say anybody did. Our feet were wet. Our eyebrows were sweaty, full of prickly heat from the K-pots. It was hard to move, but fear kept us going. I did have the feeling that I was not going to live through this night. That is what pushed us forward. Right after the firefight, I knew we were going to have to walk back. I knew they weren't going to provide us with air support. I was kind of used to it because of our C-O."
Specialist Christopher Quinalty, 2nd Platoon, A/1/32.

Black on Everything

Barclay looked around at his soldiers and knew most of his NCO leadership was gone. Most everyone had their night vision goggles on. There were only nine of them now, eleven with the Terp and the THT soldier. Everyone was afraid. Their perimeter was collapsed, and everyone was nearly foot to foot when lying prone. Hang had no M-203 rounds left. He had fired 36. Duncan had fifty rounds left for his M-240B machinegun. He had fired 950 rounds. Bratland was down to one mag for his M-4. Quinalty was on his last drum for his M-249 SAW. He had fired over 600 rounds. Caracciolo had nine M-203 rounds left. He had fired sixteen. Everyone was in a similar state. If it weren't for Gordon's and Yusella's ammo, most of them would have been down to fewer than one magazine except for Caracciolo and Hang, who still had most of their M-4 rounds.

"Sir," said Marchetti, "I couldn't find my aid bag. I went down a ways. I don't know where it is."

"Screw it," said Yusella, "we're not going down for it." The bag could have been blown all the way down to the riverbed, and the enemy could be down there. It wasn't worth it. Barclay felt the same, or maybe it was that he had too many other things on his mind. Barclay was still in coms with higher. He gave Attack Six a SITREP.

Hang looked around at his fellow soldiers and thought, "We have to get off this spur as soon as possible. There is no fuckin' way I'm dying on this mountain."

Bratland listened as his PL explained to McKnight how they were black on ammo, water, and personnel. Barclay asked Attack Six, "Will the Q-R-F be able to come to us, or do we have to make it back to the Q-R-F?"

"Stay on mission," replied Attack Six. "Continue to Landigal in the morning."

"What the fuck?" thought Bratland in desperation. He couldn't believe it.

"Are you serious?" thought Yusella in shock. He thought he knew his CO pretty well, but he couldn't believe what McKnight had just said.

Quinalty hadn't thought his spirit could drop any further. He realized, though, that he was wrong. His heart sank when he heard that order. He wasn't surprised by it, but he was angered. He thought McKnight was completely out of touch with the reality of the situation.

Duncan had been afraid, and he still was, but now he was furious. He couldn't believe a commander could give such an order.

"Oh my God!" thought Hang fearfully. "I'm going to die!" Not thirty seconds before, he had said to himself that there was no way he was dying on this mountain. Now he was coming to terms with the reality of their situation. Everyone was extremely dejected. Everyone was afraid.

Bratland heard Barclay say, "Everyone stay put." Then Barclay walked off into the darkness by himself with his MBITR. Bratland figured Barclay did not want his soldiers to see their leadership arguing.

LT Hewerdine's ANA QRF; North of Donga:

"That's bullshit!" seethed Hewerdine when he overheard McKnight give Barclay the order to remain on mission.

"Fuck that! Fuck this!" He had been monitoring events all night on the Attack channel and could not believe a commander could order such a small patrol to remain on mission in such a bad place, black on ammo and water as they were. On top of that, Barclay had the wounded MEDEVAC-ed out. Hewerdine thought the enemy had to know Barclay's exact location. All they had to do was watch where the Blackhawks had hovered, and they'd know right where the position was.

Seething at the order to keep the patrol on mission, Hewerdine was glad he had not called back to let them know where his element was. What happened to Barclay's patrol was precisely the reason he had not called in to notify Attack Main of his ANA element. He was worried they might make him do something similar.

Now that the helicopters were gone, Hewerdine considered moving forward again. He motioned to his ANA and got up slowly. The Afghans followed. They began working their way slowly south along the riverbed.

LT Barclay's Patrol; Spur North of Landigal:

Barclay was gone, and the others lay prone or sat in an out-facing perimeter in the darkness. Quinalty thought about the order to remain on mission, and questions flashed across his mind one after another.

"Do we have the ammo? Do we have the water? Do we have the resources? Do we have the energy?" Then that little bit of reasoning slammed shut with reality, and he thought just as quickly, "Doesn't matter—irrelevant—push forward; those are the orders."

The big Texan thought about what he would do when he ran out of ammo. He would fight with whatever he had, and when he had nothing left, he would use his teeth. Quinalty had never been more afraid. He glanced at some of the others and thought they looked terrified or in shock. Then he saw Marchetti and thought the medic looked okay. Quinalty liked Marchetti. The medic was one of those guys who always had a positive disposition. Quinalty always admired that about Marchetti, how he could take a bad situation and make it good. Marchetti had always been somewhat reserved when it came to interaction and stayed with the people with whom he was directly involved in the PL's HQ section, but Quinalty liked him and thought the medic was a friendly guy. He was a great medic.

Quinalty knew Barclay had moved off to talk to McKnight, but he figured they would have to stay on mission. That was the last thing he wanted to do, but he felt he knew their CO. In his opinion, McKnight had shown over and over that the mission was more important than the man.

Yusella was passing out ammunition. He still had a number of mags and knew the others were almost out. Everyone was scared, and being low on ammo only made them that much more anxious.

"What the fuck?" said Duncan to Yusella. "I just saw a flash over there."

"Where?"

"Right over there!"

"I didn't see anything."

"There's another one. Right there! Did you see that flash?"

"No."

Everyone was looking around them. No one saw any flashes. Duncan was nervous. How could the others not see them? He kept seeing flashes. After several more times they realized Duncan's night vision was malfunctioning. He had to take his off.

After a while Barclay came back[xxiii] and said quietly but forcefully, "Get your shit! Ruck up! Let's go! Keep it tight. The Q-R-F can't come to us, so we have to go down to the riverbed and walk out."

He then told Yusella and Duncan, his corporals and the highest-ranking men he had left, to keep their formation tight and keep everyone together. Barclay briefed them on what guys needed to do, where they needed to be, and how they were going to get out of there. Barclay made sure the weapons, equipment, and rucks of the four wounded men were distributed evenly among the remaining men. Then, satisfied that they were as prepared as they were going to be, he said, "Let's go!" and started down.

Barclay led them down the finger (the easier route, which they had decided against taking when they ascended the spur before dusk) because he knew going down the steep face of the spur would be extremely dangerous in the dark. Even with

128

night vision on, they couldn't see well. And although they had fired much of their ammo, they were heavily laden carrying the additional weight of the weapons and equipment of four wounded men.

Barclay was leading the group down the side of the spur, but at the same time he was trying to keep his soldiers together. Every time he looked back, he saw men falling down, rolling ankles, and fighting to keep their balance. Barclay could smell ammonia off his own body because his muscles were burning. Every man on his patrol was burning thousands of calories but had only taken in a few hundred. Barclay hoped their water would hold out. They had brought enough for three days, but they hadn't counted on such exertion. He was already getting low, and so were the others.

Yusella heard someone behind him say, "Slow down! Slow down!"

"I'm not slowing down," he said. "Keep up!"

Barclay tried to lead them over the best possible ground where there was good footing, but spots he had thought looked solid gave beneath his 230 pounds. He would slip and barely catch himself. Others were not so lucky and fell or slid down into holly bushes or boulders. Barclay could barely see, and he was the point man. It occurred to him that he was the PL and should not be on point, but the situation was so bad that there was no other way. He just kept looking down at his GPS, using it to guide where they were going.

Hang was in the rear position. He moved down the spur, constantly turning to look behind him and to the sides. He was slipping a lot because of it. Several times he had to walk backwards. The extra pack and equipment of the wounded made it even worse.

Barclay never realized how much he missed his sergeants until right at that moment. He had everyone in single file. He could see the QRF strobes high up across the valley. It would just take a while to climb down the east side of the valley, move north along the riverbed, and then climb up to them atop the west side. It was four, maybe five, klicks back to the road where the QRF element was waiting to meet them.

129

Quinalty had never known fear in such magnitude before. He did not expect to live through the night. He didn't know it, but Bratland felt the same way, as well as Duncan, Caracciolo, Hang, Yusella, and probably most of the others. His feet were wet with sweat. It was hot, and they had been exerting themselves for hours. Quinalty wiped the sweat from his eyes. His K-pot was heavy and hot. Sweat poured down his face. Fear was the common denominator that kept everyone going.

SFC North's QRF: Through his night vision goggles Lomen watched Barclay's IR strobes slowly working their way down the far valley. They were moving painfully slow. Lomen felt bad for them. There couldn't be many of them left. Lomen knew the patrol had left with only thirteen soldiers. Now they were down to nine—not many in enemy territory. He wondered about their ammo situation. He hoped they could make it back without tripping another ambush. He knew the QRF was at least in a position to support them if they did. Then Lomen saw the strobes stop descending and begin moving laterally to their left. It was barely perceptible because the column was moving so slowly, but Lomen could tell Barclay's patrol was down off the side of the spur now and moving through the riverbed.

LT Hewerdine's ANA QRF; North of Donga: Hewerdine had moved about thirty meters forward. He still monitored the Attack net and breathed with relief when he heard Barclay's patrol was finally on their way back. Hewerdine was glad McKnight finally came to his senses. In his mind Hewerdine began working out what was happening. Barclay's patrol should be working their way back to Alia Bad where they would link with the QRF. Hewerdine could not see Barclay's men, but he could see the QRF. They were just south of Alia Bad, atop the valley road. Hewerdine was just north of Donga, along the riverbed. Donga and Alia Bad were opposite each other across the valley.

Hewerdine was trying to decide what to do. He had begun to realize how rash it had been for him to run out into the valley with only five ANA.

"I don't need to be here any longer," he said to himself. "The enemy has fled. The MEDEVAC is gone. The craziness has stopped. The Q-R-F is in position." Hewerdine decided to turn back. If he moved forward, it could end in a friendly-fire incident. The QRF could mistake them for insurgents, or Barclay's men could. He decided to return to the KOP. He motioned for his ANA to turn back and then headed back north along the riverbed.

LT Barclay's Patrol: Caracciolo was tired and dehydrated. He made it to the riverbed without falling and felt good about that. Everyone else had been slipping and sliding. Caracciolo began to relax. He started walking more easily and accidentally put his foot wrong. He tripped on a rock and went down hard, twisting his ankle. He got up and continued on, limping in pain, but he couldn't keep pace and was falling behind.

Barclay was still on point, several men ahead of him. Caracciolo saw him look back. Barclay used the IR flash on his nods to get everyone's attention, and when they looked forward he gave the hand signal to stop. Then he moved back to Caracciolo.

"Why are you moving so slow?" he whispered in the soundless night.

"I twisted my ankle, sir." Caracciolo answered as softly as he could. Everyone knew the enemy could be anywhere in the darkness around them. They'd been surrounded on three sides and were trying to walk out through an area from which they had taken fire.

"Do you need to stop?"

"No." Caracciolo wanted desperately to stop, but he didn't want to slow them down. He was still an FNG and didn't want everybody saying, "It's the new guy; we gotta wait for him." Also, for his own livelihood, Caracciolo knew they needed to get to the QRF vehicles as soon as possible.

"Well, pick it up," said Barclay. "Our patrol is starting to get separated." Barclay knew everyone was exhausted. They had humped the valley that day, fought a battle, suffered casualties, were low on ammo, felt dehydrated, and now were

131

fighting the emotional strain of moving in the dark through an enemy area.

Bratland was convinced that somewhere between them and the QRF element were ACM waiting to ambush them. Bratland didn't know about anyone else, but he was scared. He had seen how many enemy muzzle flashes there were (a lot more than they had), knew they had only two mags per man left, and had four klicks to walk in the heart of bad-guy land at night. Bratland did not think he was going to live to see sunrise.

"This is fuckin' bullshit!" he said aloud in frustration. "We don't have enough rounds right now to kill a fuckin' goat, let alone the enemy in a fight."

Bratland could tell Barclay was fed up and didn't want to hear it because his LT turned around and snapped, "Scrappy, just shut the fuck up and do it."[xxiv]

Yusella heard someone behind him fall. Whoever it was, their weapon clanged against rock, and there was an audible "Fuck!"

"Be quiet," snapped Yusella. He was afraid they'd be ambushed. They were making too much noise as they stumbled blindly along in the darkness. "If anyone's waiting in ambush," he thought, "we'll be annihilated!"

Hang was still in the rear, constantly looking to the sides and back. He could see the QRF strobes on the far left ridgeline. But then he noticed something on the top right ridgeline. He could see several silhouettes of men. He didn't know how many were up there, but there was at least a half-squad.

"I see people!" Hang hissed forward. "I see people!" He told the men in front of him to let Barclay know about the figures on the top right ridgeline.

Barclay took the information and sized up their situation.

"If we get hit in this valley while they are on top of us, we are screwed." With that in mind, he gave a flash with his GCP and called up to North to make sure the QRF still had eyes on them.

"Attack Two-Seven, can you see us?"

132

SFC North's QRF: North, Lomen, Wilkinson, and the others were in position atop the valley. They were still in perimeter defense centered on their vehicles. North and Lomen had visually been monitoring Barclay's withdrawal because they could see the strobes. However, once Barclay got down in the valley, the closer they got, the harder it was to keep eyes on.

The QRF had their own strobes out and figured Barclay's men could see them. They heard Barclay ask whether they had eyes on and replied affirmatively. North advised they just needed to keep moving north for another klick, and they'd be right below Alia Bad. Then they could start their ascent up.

Lomen moved around and made sure his squad was staying alert. They had been hit three times on the way there, so obviously bad guys were in the area, and the insurgents who had fired on Barclay's patrol were between the two groups. They needed to expect additional contact. This was still the worst area in the valley. The farther south they went, the worse it got.

LT Preston's First Platoon; Kandigal: Preston and Rush were worried about Barclay's patrol. From all they'd heard, it had been a hell of a TIC. And they still weren't out of danger yet. Things were quiet in their area, but the 2nd Platoon guys were in a bad place. It was frustrating not to be able to help them. The same thing had happened more than a month before in the exact same area. Then Sergeant Durgin, one of their snipers, had taken a six-man team into the area around Landigal in hopes of taking out some bad guys. Only, it had been Durgin and his team that were ambushed. Durgin had been on point and walked right into a number of insurgents.

Preston and Rush knew what a nightmare it was trying to fight the enemy in their own backyard, in the very hills where they had grown up. When that action had happened, Preston had been out on patrol at the same time and had tried to get to Durgin's team to help, but Preston and his soldiers got stuck on a cliff face a thousand feet up and were unable to get through. They had to backtrack, and by that time it was all over.

McQuade had been out on patrol, too. In fact, when that occurred several months back, McQuade had been in Darbat having Chai tea with the village elder there, a man named Haji Jamil, whom McQuade knew to be a bad guy on their list. However, McQuade had built rapport with Jamil—so much so that he could sit and have tea with him, something Jamil would not allow anyone else. When the gunfire broke out, McQuade was sitting with Jamil on his porch. McQuade heard the distant gunfire and looked off toward the sound of the fighting. Then he looked back at Jamil. The Korangali smiled. McQuade had his Terp ask Jamil, "Do you know what is going on?"

"Do not worry about it," said Jamil. "I'm sure it is nothing."

"Are you sure?" said McQuade. "There is a lot of shooting down here."

"There is only shooting when you come here."

McQuade told his men to move out. Unfortunately it took more than an hour before they reached Durgin's team up on the mountain—not in time to save the sergeant.

Durgin had been extremely well liked. Preston and Rush remembered a time they had been out with Durgin in early June. The sniper had been assigned to their platoon. They had stopped during a night march and were deciding their next move. Preston and Rush were talking among themselves, being the platoon leader and platoon sergeant. Rush had totally forgotten Durgin was accompanying their platoon because the snipers were only attached to patrols for missions. When a figure walked up and stood next to them while they were talking, Rush thought it was one of his privates coming over to listen in.

"What the fuck do you think you're doing?" he spat. He couldn't see who it was in the dark, but he was going to chew his ass for stepping out of line. "Who the fuck do you think you are?"

"Sorry, Sergeant," said the voice apologetically, backing up quickly and starting to turn away, "I was just . . ."

"Wait," said Rush. "Who is that? Durgin? Oh, I'm sorry, brother! I didn't know it was you. I thought it was one of my soldiers."

Preston was roaring with laughter. Both Durgin and Rush were, too. It was something they joked about right up until 13 June, when Durgin was KIA near Landigal. Now it was August, and Rush had a lot of friends in the 2nd Platoon at very nearly the same spot. He hoped they'd be okay.

LT Barclay's Patrol: "We need water, ammo, rest," said Bratland bitterly; he was furious with their company commander for putting them in their present situation. "We need . . ."

"I don't want to hear it," snapped Barclay.

It seemed to Duncan it was taking all night to get back. There was no illumination, and he worried every step led them closer to an ambush. They could see with their night vision but not very well and not very far. It was the worst walk of Duncan's life.

"Hey, sir," asked Bratland to his CO, "if we get hit, can the Q-R-F even cover us?"

Barclay also worried about an ambush. He was in coms with North and asked his platoon sergeant to fire some fifty-caliber suppressive fire against the east side of the valley. This was partly harassing fire in case anyone was still over there, and at the same time it was to let them know if they opened up on the patrol, they would get .50 calibers, M-203, and MK-19 return fire from the high ground across the valley.

Everyone could see the tracers from the fifty spitting across the valley. There was something comforting about the sound of a fifty-caliber machinegun. No enemy weapon sounded like it.

The QRF didn't look to be too much farther ahead. However, everyone knew visual distance was misleading in the mountains. North's QRF was maybe only a klick ahead, but in the terrain where they were located, that may as well be three klicks. Everyone's boots were sinking in the silt of the riverbed, and it was like walking on a beach in soft sand.

However, the alternative of walking on the rocky side was much worse.

Hang kept looking to his side and rear. He kept thinking, "I hope Sergeant Gean is okay." He could hear the others asking whether anyone had water. Hang still had almost a camelback of water.

"I do," he said, taking a big drink. Then Duncan came over and pulled the camelback to his mouth. He started drinking it down.

"Chill on the water!" said Hang as Duncan sucked it down. "Sip on it, don't fuckin' chug it!" It was too late. Duncan drank, and so did Quinalty and several others. Hang noticed the bigger guys needed to drink the most water. When they handed him his camelback, it was empty.

"Fuuuck!"

Asadabad: Gean regained consciousness as he was pulled out of the helicopter. He found himself at a medical treatment facility surrounded by doctors and nurses. He looked over and saw Bleidorn. His friend was on a gurney, still screaming because he was in so much pain. Medical personnel surrounded Bleidorn, as well.

"Ben, how you doin' buddy?"

"I'm okay. You all right?"

The doctors were treating their wounds, but it seemed to both Gean and Bleidorn they were poking and prodding carelessly because everything was a new experience in agony. But it wasn't their own pain that bothered them so much. It was hearing their friends. Bleidorn heard Gean scream in pain.

"YOU OKAY?"

"AAAGGGHHH," cried Gean.

"YOU'RE HURTING HIM!" bellowed Bleidorn. "STOP FUCKIN' HURTING HIM!"

Bleidorn could hear them talking about Gean. They were saying he was paralyzed and had been since the moment the bullet struck him.

"NO!" he said to get their attention. "He used his leg. I saw him use his leg when I was carrying him."

Then a medic grabbed Bleidorn's knee.

"AAAAAGGGGHHH!" Bleidorn rose up and swung with all his might. The medic reeled back just in time to avoid the punch, and Bleidorn's fist missed by less than an inch. Bleidorn fell back down to the gurney screaming in pain.

"BEN? YOU ALRIGHT?" shouted Gean, enraged. He couldn't understand why they kept hurting Bleidorn. "WHAT THE FUCK?"

Bleidorn's punch had been too much for the medical personnel. The big sergeant could have seriously hurt their medic. From that moment on, Bleidorn was sedated. Gean saw his friend was unconscious and was grateful Bleidorn was no longer in pain.

"Where am I?" asked Gean.

"Asadabad. What's your name?"

"Sergeant Chase Gean."

They kept asking him questions. Gean didn't know if they were trying to keep his mind off his injuries or if they were just insatiably curious, but they wouldn't stop. Then one of them asked, "Who was your medic?"

"My medic was Doc Marchetti."

"Marchetti? I know him." The doctor knew Marchetti and spoke highly of him, describing him and the type of man he was. That helped, and Gean began to trust the man because he thought so highly of Marchetti.

"Do you want to make a phone call?"

"Yes," replied Gean. "I want to call my girlfriend, Shannon."

Bagram; Kabul: Gordon arrived at Bagram with Reyna. The first thing he did was ask about Gean and Bleidorn. The medics didn't have a clue what he was talking about. Gordon explained that two of their soldiers had been MEDEVAC-ed out before him. They should have been there at least fifteen minutes prior to their arrival. He asked again where they were. The medics didn't know and didn't seem to care. They tried to take Gordon's boot off, but the FO was furious at their flippant attitude.

"You're not touching me till I find Chase and Ben. Their bird left a half hour before ours did. They gotta be here. You're not fuckin' touching me till I find out where my friends are."

A doctor was there preparing to examine Gordon's gunshot wound. He told Gordon he would look into it. The doctor walked over and made a phone call. He got off the phone and told Gordon the other Blackhawk had stopped in Asadabad because of the severity of the wounds. The two soldiers had needed immediate care.

Gordon had known how badly Gean was hit. He had been worried his friend was going to bleed to death on the side of their spur. He now realized Gordon's femoral artery might have been hit. He feared one or both of his friends might bleed out. The uncertainty was terrible.

The KOP; Attack Main TOC:

"Why are they coming back in?" asked the BC. He called again to talk to McKnight. "I thought they were going to continue mission."

"They are out of ammo and water."

McKnight was on the landline phone with his battalion commander. The BC had just called, and, needless to say, he was not happy with the outcome of the action.

"You just got your butt kicked," he said. "What are you going to do about it?"

"Uh . . ." said McKnight, somewhat at a loss. He knew Landigal was out of the question, as, for the time being, they simply did not have the assets. But he knew they had to do something. They couldn't let the local population think the enemy had won a victory over them.

"Well," he said, "we've got to do something to take the fight back to the enemy."

"That's exactly what you need to do. What are you going to do?"

"Uh . . . cordon search Alia Bad?"

"That's exactly what you need to do."

McKnight got off the phone. He knew he was not in a popularity contest. He was in command. McKnight called

North and said, "Hey, I want you guys to search the Alia Bad area because that is one of the areas they would have gone to as they came down the streambed. Cordon search the village. Send out an element to do a B-D-A assessment."[xxv]

Stevens was beside McKnight when he issued the order. Stevens was not at all surprised. He knew his CO. He felt McKnight's typical response to exhausted patrols was "Suck it up and drive on! Ruck that ranger tab!"[xxvi]

LT Hewerdine's ANA QRF; South of O-P-Three:
Hewerdine and his Afghans reached the KOP outer-perimeter and identified themselves to the ANA sentries at O-P-3. Then they crossed the wire and moved up to the ANA positions. Hewerdine dropped off the five ANA soldiers and returned to the ETT hooch. He was exhausted. He kept his radio on the Attack net and lay down on his cot. He passed out listening to the QRF updates to Attack Main.

LT Barclay's Patrol: Barclay estimated they had moved another klick down the valley. He figured they were right under the QRF. Because they were so close, and the valley was so steep, they had lost sight of the strobes. Barclay called North and asked him for more covering fire with the fifty-cal and MK-19. He wanted the fire to hit the opposite valley directly across from the QRF, with two reasons in mind: One, that would pinpoint the QRF's location, and, two, if any enemy soldiers were waiting to hit them, they would see what kind of firepower would be striking back at them from the high ground.

Within a few seconds of the request, tracers knifed across the valley passing directly over their heads. Satisfied they were where he thought they were, Barclay knew that now all they had to do was climb up to the QRF.

It wasn't straight up, but it seemed to the exhausted soldiers as though it were. There was no trail up the side of the valley that they could see. They were below a village that was cut into farming terraces. By day the terraces looked to be only four or five feet tall. However, standing in front of them, Barclay's soldiers found them to be much bigger. They slowly began to work their way up the terraces one by one.

Ocompo, Duncan, Marchetti, and Hang were behind the Terp. They brought up the tail end of the column. The Terp didn't have night vision. In his weariness, he slowed. The Americans stumbling behind him in exhaustion didn't notice. Then the Terp suddenly realized they were separated from the column. In great fear he told his American counterparts.

"Shit!" said Duncan. He had no idea how far they were from the others. The QRF was up on the road. He knew that because he could just see the strobe that was above them on the highest terrace. He decided they should start climbing. Duncan and the others started straight up. The first terrace was about twenty feet across and came to a stone back wall about eight feet tall. Duncan pulled himself up to the next terrace and then did it again. The terraces had corn, but the corn didn't remind him of Iowa one bit. The Korangalis didn't cultivate row crops. It didn't look anything like what Duncan was used to seeing back home.

Barclay was still leading the patrol. Barclay was exhausted, but it was still easier for him to pull up someone like Bratland than the other way around. Barclay helped his RTO up, then Caracciolo, Quinalty, Yusella, and the THT. He put his hand down for the next man and looked, but he didn't see him.

"Shit!" he said to himself, realizing their patrol had been separated. That was when Barclay missed his NCOs the most. He was having to micromanage everything, and the strain was exhausting. Now their column was separated. It seemed to him he had checked their line several minutes ago, so he didn't think they could be far. He told the column to hold up while he went back down and looked for Duncan and the others.

Duncan knew there was a path and figured the LT and the others must have found it. He figured it was their bad luck to have been separated and have to climb up the hard way. Duncan walked along the terrace trying to find a trail. He couldn't see any sign of the others, but he could see the QRF strobe up top.

140

Barclay found the separated group and had them link back up with the main body. Barclay knew his men were exhausted. He feared they would lose someone as a heat casualty and wondered how they would get that man up. Only, somehow his men kept going. The few men that had any remaining water shared it with the men who were worst off, and they all kept going. Everyone knew the QRF on the road above would have as much water as they could drink in their trucks. They just needed to reach them.

Duncan thought the strobes above looked close. But with every terrace they climbed, it didn't seem they were getting any closer. It was agony. Duncan had never been so thirsty.

The terraces were high; even the shortest ones were six feet. The patrol had to zigzag and work its way up each one. The soldiers had to help the man in front and then stop and pull up the man behind. Barclay was exhausted and knew his men were in even worse shape than he was. He had only made it up a few of the terraces before he called North and asked him to send down an element to link up with them. The fresh troops could assist them in getting their gear up the rest of the way.

SFC North's QRF: North called over to Lomen and told him to take an element down to Barclay's patrol. Lomen got Wilkinson, and they grabbed several bottles of water each. Then they started down. Lomen was shocked to find the terraces no less than eight feet tall. Some of them were ten feet. He and Wilkinson had to work their way down carefully to make sure they didn't fall and get hurt themselves.

HMMWVs just outside the KOP wire (photo by SGT Leroy Strickland)

"They looked like hell! They were carrying each other's gear; they had to carry the leftover stuff from the wounded. At one point I ended up climbing down. There were big, ten- to twelve-foot terraces. I think I climbed down with Wilky— Shane Wilkinson—to help them climb back up. They were beat tired! They were using their rifles as walking sticks. They were so tired they couldn't hold themselves up anymore. They were crazy beat! To watch them carry everyone else's gear up the mountain, I felt so bad for them. I'm thinking it's bullshit that they have to search the village. They've been up all night, lost four guys in a firefight, they are exhausted, and now they have to search the village. Second Squad got blasted."
Sergeant Josh Lomen, Squad Leader, 3rd Squad, 2nd Platoon, A/1/32.

Cordon Search

Barclay's patrol was exhausted. None of them had ever been so tired in their entire lives. The terraces were vertical. They worked their way from one terraced paddy to the next, slowly but inexorably dragging themselves up to the road atop the side of the valley. Many times the terraces were too high, over ten feet, and they had to move laterally until they found an irrigation lane where they could climb to the next one.

They weren't halfway up when Duncan vomited. He looked at the others, and it seemed everyone was throwing up. Duncan had never been more spent. He could tell it was almost dawn. It occurred to him he'd been up since before dawn the day before.

Quinalty was so heavy that wherever he stepped, the ground just crumbled, and he slid back. He was exhausted and dehydrated and didn't know who was in front of him or who was behind him. Everyone was helping each other. That was the only way they were able to ascend the terraces. The man in front would help pull up the man behind him. Then that man would turn around and assist whoever was behind him.

Caracciolo looked up and then back down. He figured they were about halfway. A rare few were mumbling and cursing in exhausted frustration, but most of them just gasped for oxygen and tried to keep moving. To Caracciolo, when he first saw the terraces before dusk yesterday, they looked to be only waist high. But when he got right next to them, even the shortest one was taller than he was. They climbed, moved laterally to find a spot with a ledge or a handhold, and then climbed again. Someone found a trail along the side, but it was steep and loose. The bigger guys constantly fell or slid back as the ground gave way beneath them. The average Afghan farmer's weight was no more than 160 pounds at the most. Quinalty, Barclay, and Duncan weighed 300 pounds each with their weapons, body armor, and additional gear from the wounded.

Caracciolo was so tired that he was staggering. His ankle was swollen and throbbing from when he'd sprained it in the riverbed a few hours ago. He was thirsty. He had drained his camelback and a two-quart canteen of water, and he didn't have any more. He tried to rationalize that such a fact was good, in that he wasn't carrying the weight anymore. It also dawned on him that he had fired sixteen M-203 rounds, so that weight was gone as well. However, that bit of reasoning was stamped out when he realized he was carrying the additional weight of one of the wounded men's ruck and weapon. His load had never felt heavier.

Then, suddenly, Barclay heard Lomen call down to him.

"Thank God," said Barclay. The sun was just casting its light in the eastern skies. They linked up with Lomen and Wilkinson in the middle of the terraces. The sun wasn't visible, but the distant sky had an orange hue that signaled dawn. There was an abandoned house along the midway point in the side of the valley. It was below the rest of Alia Bad. It was one of several and was four or five fingers away from the *Y* intersect.

Hang was beside Duncan when they saw Lomen on the terraces above them. It was the greatest morale boost Hang had ever felt to date.

"Grab this stuff!" said Hang, holding up the extra pack he was carrying. "Grab this."

"Hey," he heard Lomen call down angrily. He was looking at Duncan. "Get that weapon up!" Hang looked to his side and saw Duncan using the M-240B as a crutch. Duncan either didn't hear him or didn't care. He kept using it to hold himself up. Hang had difficulty swallowing. His tongue was so swollen that he couldn't speak normally. He had never been thirstier in his life.

When Bratland climbed up and saw Lomen and Wilkinson, he realized they were going to make it. He almost relaxed except that he knew they were only halfway up and still had to climb the rest of the way. Lomen had been Bratland's squad leader before he had become Barclay's RTO, so Bratland knew both men well.

"Scrap," said Lomen, looking at Bratland, "what the fuck happened? You look like shit!"

Bratland just wanted to be by himself, away from everyone, away from conversation. Then Lomen said, "Hey, we got fresh mags for you guys. Switch 'em out. Reload." Lomen and Wilkinson began handing out water and taking the extra rucks to help carry equipment and ease the load on the obviously exhausted patrol.

They continued the climb. It took at least another half hour before the first man reached the top. As he did, the first slivers of light peeked over the top of the mountain.

Caracciolo climbed up and stood among the others on the top of the road. He had thought they'd never get there. He looked at the eastern horizon and saw the sun starting its slow climb.

"We got shot right before the sun went down," he thought to himself, "and now we get back as the sun is coming up."

Yusella and Quinalty were on the last terrace. Yusella knew he was spent. He was so tired he couldn't think straight. Yusella saw Quinalty wedge his SAW in the dirt atop the road and use it for leverage to pull himself up. Then he heard someone atop the road yelling at Quinalty saying, "Hey, don't you fuckin' treat your weapon like that!"

Yusella didn't think Quinalty even heard the guy. Yusella didn't care. "Get up there, man," he said to Quinalty.

When Duncan finally reached the terrace where Lomen and Wilkinson were, it was as if every bit of remaining energy drained out of his body. Duncan stood in a daze as they handed him water and ammo. Duncan looked up and saw SFC North farther up. He was on the radio ready to go with everyone in full battle rattle. Duncan climbed up a few more terraces and saw the trucks were staged and waiting. They were providing over-watch with a soldier manning each turret weapon.

Someone took Duncan's ruck while someone else took his M-240B. Duncan took a drink of water and promptly vomited. Then he climbed the last terrace and reached the vehicles. Duncan looked at the rising sun, and somehow the daylight surprised him.

Once atop the road, Lomen said, "We are searching the village door to door. McKnight wants us to search this whole fuckin' village. So let's get to it."

"You've got to be fuckin' kidding me," said Bratland to himself. "We've been up for more than thirty-six hours, and you expect us to do this without sleep, without eating, without cleaning our weapons." Bratland seethed at McKnight's order. "This guy's a fucking psycho! He's trying to get us all killed."

"Bullshit," said Quinalty to himself when he heard the order to search the village. "Bullshit!" Then the soldier in him said, "Whatever. Got to be done." Quinalty knew they couldn't say anything. What could any of them do? Because of their level of understanding, nothing any of them could say would change the outcome. It would be up to those in charge of them to change the outcome.

Caracciolo was shocked when he heard their CO still wanted them to search the village. His shock turned quickly to anger. "What's your problem?" he thought of McKnight. "We just walked all night. We are tired. We took four casualties. And you want us to do this—still!" Caracciolo always heard the others bad mouthing McKnight, but until that very moment, he never understood it. Caracciolo was new to A Company, but he had spoken to McKnight several times and thought his CO was a pretty nice guy. However, he felt this was too much. For the first time, he thought he saw what the others were always complaining about.

Yusella stood as if in a dream. He was so tired he had trouble thinking. When he heard the initial order to cordon and

146

search the village, he almost swung on the voice that had relayed McKnight's order. He had nearly thrown the punch and only just stopped himself.

Bratland, too, went through his own rationalization: what he thought was idiocy regarding who they were and what was expected of them. They were professional soldiers. They were the 1st of the 32nd, the Chosin battalion, the Chosin soldiers. They were Alpha Company. They believed they were the best of the best in the US Army, the most powerful military force the world had ever seen—from their origin in Hawaii guarding the Queen's Palace to the Battle of the Chosin Reservoir during the Korean War, all the way to present day. Bratland knew they just needed to bite their tongues and just deal with it whether they liked it or not. But he didn't like it.

Bratland exchanged glances with both Barclay and Lomen. Then Barclay said, "Brat, just take a seat in the Humvee and get some sleep. We're going to rotate out. Third squad is going to search the place."

Caracciolo was grateful to 3rd Squad. They pretty much told the 2nd Squad guys to get in the vehicles and pull security as they searched the village. They knew how tired 2nd Squad was.

It had been a long, terrifying night. Duncan walked over and got behind the trucks. He sat down and lit up a cigarette. They gave Duncan food, but he didn't eat. He just drank water. This time, since Duncan had been able to catch his breath, the water stayed in his stomach. Duncan took about two minutes of rest before he went up into the turret of a HMMWV and got behind the M-240B, relieving "Blue" Blake. Everyone called Blake "Blue" because of the movie *Old School*. In the movie, a man about seventy years old named Blue pledges the fraternity house among a bunch of younger men. Although Joseph Blake wasn't eighty, he had enlisted as a private in his early thirties, so he may as well have been eighty as far as his eighteen- and nineteen-year-old fellow enlistees were concerned. The age difference earned him the name "Blue" to his fellow soldiers.

Blake moved over to North's waiting group. Duncan and the other soldiers of Barclay's patrol provided over-watch while North's men moved out to do a cordon search of the village. North led Lomen's squad down the valley toward the village. They descended a little goat trail that led to the river bottom below, and then they started up the opposite side. It took almost an hour for them to reach the far village. Lomen was directing his squad as they searched the hooches and shanties, while Barclay, back at the HMMWVs, manned the radio. At that point, Barclay felt a sense of relief.

"Thank God it's finally over."

Bratland and the others were in the HMMWVs. They pulled security and took turns sleeping for twenty minutes at a time. They didn't know how long they were going to be there, and the power naps could keep them going. Bratland refilled all his magazines, refilled all his water bottles, canteens, and camelbacks, and even took a nap. He actually woke up refreshed and ready to go.

Hang didn't even try to take a nap. His eyes hurt, his tongue was still swollen, and he had a headache from being overly tired; he was still too keyed up from the night before, however, and didn't feel they were safe yet. Hang didn't think they would be safe until they got back to the KOP. He sat in the turret of one of the HMMWVs and kept his eyes on 3rd Squad and any place from which he thought the enemy might try to sneak up on them.

While searching the village, Lomen's squad found one man who was on their wanted list. They arrested him, zip-tied him, and walked him back up to their waiting trucks where they put him in one of the HMMWVs.

Then they loaded back up and started back for the KOP. Barclay was dead tired, but he knew he still had an AAR and a debrief when he got back. Bratland suddenly thought, "Those fuckers ain't going to let us get back. They've got us beat down, they've got us worn out, and they just watched us search this village. They are going to rocket us on the way back."

They didn't. The HMMWVs made it back without incident. They drove through the KOP concertina wire just after 1200, 24 hours after they had left it the day before.

When they got back inside the safety of the KOP, Caracciolo went to his tent and put his assault pack down.

148

When he did, he saw it was covered in blood. He remembered using it to elevate Bleidorn's leg. The reality of that was as if someone had slapped him.

Yusella still felt as though he was walking around in a dream. He expected Gean to come over and give him a debrief but realized he didn't have a squad leader anymore. Yusella turned to Caracciolo and Quinalty and said, "Clean your weapons."

Hang sat cleaning the mud from his M-4. The others were on their cots or outside doing the same with their weapons. Hang's M-4 was caked with mud and the dust-like powder that seemed to be ubiquitous in the Korangal.

"That mission was useless," he thought. "We never even reached Landigal."

Duncan sat on his cot and chain smoked a pack of cigarettes. He thought about the long night and the loss of his close friends and seethed at the stupidity of the mission. Knowing it was over, couldn't be helped, and didn't do any good to think about, Duncan rolled into a fetal position on his cot. He was completely burned out and quickly fell asleep.

Barclay went to the TOC for a debrief with McKnight. For Barclay, the debrief was a little disconcerting. He told McKnight what he thought about what had happened and what he thought they could do to improve on their next mission. Barclay knew there was no use bringing up anything other than business. McKnight[xxvii] was all about the mission and business, so Barclay treated it as such. Barclay explained why four of his soldiers were wounded and left it at that. It was another day.

When the debrief ended, Barclay went to get something to eat and find out how his men were doing. Everyone was going through their own wind-down process. Some were already asleep. Barclay felt the need to be clean. He went over to the area where they showered and lifted the five-gallon jug up to the container with the shower head. He filled it with his five gallons and then stripped down to get beneath the nozzle. He opened it up and felt the tiny stream of cold liquid temporarily jar the fatigue from his exhausted body. He knew he needed to get some sleep, but he also wanted to call his wife and let her know he was okay.

"Those Tenth Mountain guys of Attack Company deserve all the credit they can get. Those guys fought hard! You couldn't ask more from American soldiers." Lieutenant Daniel Hewerdine, ETT, Korangal Outpost.

After Landigal

Jae Barclay was in the Korangal Valley for only sixteen more days. On day sixteen, Barclay was in a HMMWV moving up the KOP road from Kandigal when his vehicle hit an IED. Of the five soldiers in the HMMWV, three were KIA. Barclay survived the horrific blast but was so badly wounded that he did not return to his unit. Barclay was promoted to captain but was medically discharged from the military. He now lives with his wife and two children in Huntsville, Alabama.

Ben Bleidorn woke up in Asadabad. The first thing he did was ask for a phone to call his wife. He feared she might have heard about casualties and would be worrying about him. His wife, Stephanie, was pregnant and expecting their first child in early September.

"I've been shot in the leg," he told her.

"Shut up! Stop kidding around."

"I really am."

It had been only a week since her husband left home to return to his unit from leave, so Stephanie couldn't believe it.

Bleidorn's femur had been shattered into 52 pieces. Since Landigal, it has healed somewhat but is cutting away at the knee. Every time Bleidorn takes a step on his right leg, the damaged bone cuts away at his knee. Bleidorn is medically retired from the military. He still has his leg, but he walks with a permanent limp and says that "they are just basically waiting for it to go bad."

Bleidorn's knee was scoped in 2009, and doctors told him there is no cartilage left. They said when it becomes too much to take, they will give him a new knee and half a femur from a cadaver. Bleidorn is supposed to use a cane, but he hates to.

"I'm too young to use a cane," said Bleidorn in his interview on 8 February 2010.

Bleidorn helps his wife take care of their daughter Madallena. She was born on 6 September with Charge Syndrome. Madallena was in the neo-natal ICU for 47 days after she was born. She is blind and partially deaf and has a low immune system. In her early days, her parents had to maintain a constant vigilance for pneumonia. Bleidorn marvels at his wife and knows how lucky he is to have married such a mentally tough, wonderful woman. After Landigal, he was in a wheelchair rolling in and out of the neo-natal ICU, his wife Stephanie Bleidorn taking care of both him and his daughter. Bleidorn received a Silver Star for valor for dragging Gean to safety under fire and continuing to fight after he was severely wounded, but he insists it's his wife Stephanie who should have received the medal for what she had been through.

Nick Bratland: Bratland's time in the Korangal ended on the same day as Barclay's: 19 August 2006. Bratland was driving the HMMWV when the IED exploded. Bratland suffered third-degree burns over 58 percent of his body. He has scarring on his face around his mouth and nose. His hands, chest, back, and right arm are badly scarred.

Because he was on such high doses of medication, Bratland had the strangest recurring dreams. The worst was a nightmare that made him wake night after night panicked and bathed in sweat. In this recurring dream, he is back in Afghanistan with his friends and family. They are under attack, getting hit with rockets and machinegun fire. Bratland's friends and family are in a boxing ring surrounded by sand bags. There is no escape, and the enemy keeps attacking them.

Bratland recovered from his wounds, although he has permanent scarring. He could have stayed in the Army in a non-combative role, but Bratland chose to get out. To Bratland, the politics were dismantling the efforts of the soldiers.

Bratland felt tired of fighting both the enemy and his own higher. He was honorably discharged from the Army and returned to South Dakota. He now lives in Groton and hopes to become a police officer.

Joshua Caracciolo finished his tour in the Korangal and saw his platoon decimated. He returned to the United States and bounced around from Fort Campbell, Kentucky, to Fort Polk, Louisiana, where he reenlisted in supply in June 2008. From there he was sent to Fort Drum, New York, and then to Fort Lee, Virginia. In August 2009 he went to JRTC (Joint Readiness Training Center) in 1st BDE in preparation for deployment to Iraq in January 2010. However, his supply unit's orders to Iraq changed, and he found himself going back to Afghanistan instead. He was redeployed on 14 March 2010 and is presently in Afghanistan. Caracciolo was trying to get back into the infantry. Caracciolo hopes to become a police officer when he gets out of the military and at one point was taking online criminal justice courses.

Bob Duncan was on route clearance the morning after Landigal. There was no rest in the Korangal for an infantryman in a line platoon. Thankfully, his platoon was able to make the patrol on 4 August without making contact with the enemy.

Soon afterward, Duncan's buddy Yusella went on leave. Possibly it was because of the horrific casualties, or possibly it was because of the strong feelings most of the soldiers held for their company commander, but Yusella did not return. No one knew what happened to him or where he went. He just didn't return. It was very hard on Duncan when Yusella never came back.

Duncan recalled, "There is definitely a sense of abandonment. We were all going through it, and we all came back, but he didn't. It was pretty hard to take."

In January, Duncan was coming back off block leave. He was flying from Kuwait, and his Battalion XO, Major Gukhiesen, was on the same flight. He asked Duncan to what company he belonged.

"A Company."

Gukhiesen then asked Duncan what he thought of CPT McKnight.

Right away a warning flag went up. It was unusual for a staff officer to ask a line infantryman a question about their CO.

"He's fine," said Duncan.

Then Duncan was surprised as the major explained to him that McKnight was not well liked at battalion. Once Duncan saw they were on the same page, he spoke more candidly.

"Well, I can understand that. Most of the guys don't like him. He leads from the rear and sits at the outpost."

The major asked a lot of questions about McKnight, to which Duncan answered honestly. Duncan did not think much of his CO and admitted he did not think the captain could read elevation lines on a map. He was constantly pushing his men to cover completely unrealistic distances. The flight ended, and Duncan thought his off-the-record conversation was in the past and forgotten. Then he headed back to the KOP.

The moment Duncan returned from R&R, 1st Sergeant Combes told him the battalion sergeant major wanted to see him. Duncan went to the sergeant major and reported in. He was surprised when the sergeant major got right in his face.

"I hear you fuckin' talked to Major Gukhiesen."

"Roger, Sergeant Major."

The sergeant major began shouting at him and reprimanding Duncan about having no loyalty. He was furious. When he finally stopped, Duncan tried to explain himself.

"I figured it was an off-the-record conversation because he said Captain McKnight isn't liked up at battalion."

"He didn't say that," spat the sergeant major. "He's up at the TOC right now. We can go ask him about it."

"Okay."

Only, the sergeant major gave no indication he was up for anything other than chewing Duncan out. It was an extreme ass-chewing, the worst Duncan had ever seen. Duncan didn't even understand half the comments the sergeant major was making. He was rambling on about what Duncan thought was nonsense. Then he got personal. He started criticizing Alpha

154

Company. He told Duncan the enemy wasn't afraid of Alpha Company in the Korangal. He said Alpha Company was getting attacked so much because they didn't listen to what CPT McKnight was telling them to do—that the men were always questioning McKnight's orders. Duncan was furious but he wisely kept his mouth shut. Duncan was yelled at like this for two hours. He knew because he had noted the time he arrived.

When the sergeant major finally tired of yelling at him, Duncan was dismissed. But the next day the sergeant major told him to pack his things. Duncan had done nothing wrong, so they couldn't punish him by taking his rank, but they did something worse. They took him away from his buddies. He was immediately shipped out of A Company and moved to Charlie Company along the Pesch under Stanton. There was nothing worse one could do to a combat soldier than to take him from his buddies.

When Duncan met Stanton and 1st SGT John Mangels, all they said was, "Welcome to Charlie Company." Duncan figured they knew he'd been shipped out as a troublemaker. Duncan was surprised when they asked him what happened. He told them, and Mangels said, "You sound like a pretty honest guy. As long as you're honest in Charlie Company, you'll do great. You're in First Platoon."

Duncan missed his buddies in A Company, but he valued his time with C Company. He was amazed when a HVT was located, and Stanton, a captain and company commander, personally led a squad-sized QRF to help destroy the target.

Duncan's deployment was extremely hard on his wife, Jaqui. Over the fifteen months Duncan was deployed, all she would hear about were the horrific A/1/32 casualties. Back in August after Landigal, she had gotten the call that Chase Gean was paralyzed. She talked to Gean in the hospital, and the first thing he asked her was whether Bob was all right. Jaqui hadn't even known her husband had been in the battle.

The psychological effect this news had on her day in and day out was terrible. This continued with each day as she heard about Joseph Blake dying on 17 August, and then Drawl,

Sitton, and Jackson on the nineteenth when Barclay and Bratland were severely wounded. It went on and on.

Duncan was gone for fifteen months. His wife was alone with their newborn son for over a year. Duncan did not see his son until the boy was over a year old.

Duncan was honorably discharged from the Army and returned to his wife and family in Iowa. He has constant lower back pain from humping eighty pounds of weapons, body armor, water, and ammunition through the valleys of the Korangal. He has worn two discs in his back down to the bone, and every day he is in discomfort. Duncan went through some psychological issues and had to receive counseling for depression and anger. He was diagnosed with PTSD. He has had a difficult time readjusting to normal life.

As Duncan himself explained: "Not a day has gone by since I've been back from Afghanistan that I don't think about something that happened over there. Everything triggers something that happened over there. Just the psychological effects alone took their toll on me and my family. It was just really hard to get over. It's something I still deal with. It will never go away. Memories like that, events like that, don't just fade away."

Duncan now lives in Iowa City with Jaqui and their two sons, Robert III and Conner. Duncan's great strength fighting through the hell of the Korangal memories was his wife. She was the one worthwhile piece of his life that kept him sane and gave him something to look forward to. It wasn't easy, and his depression almost destroyed his marriage, but the support Jaqui gave him at home enabled him to move on with his life. Not a day goes by that Duncan does not think of the hell he experienced in the Korangal Valley, and he knows he is not the person he was when he first deployed to Afghanistan, but he is grateful to his wife for her strength and love.

Chase Gean was evacuated to Landstuhl, Germany. There, the doctor removed the bullet from his spine and asked him whether he wanted to keep it. He did. It was from a PKM machinegun.

Gean lives in Tucson, Arizona. He is paralyzed from the waist down and feels constant, almost-unbearable nerve pain. He has had three surgeries with the same number of pain pumps put in, unfortunately to no avail. He is being sent to the spinal cord center in San Diego. He takes fifteen to twenty pills daily just for pain.

In late 2007, Gean felt something against the inside of his arm. He had his arm X-rayed, and a bullet was discovered. It was starting to work its way out. Gean remembered being hit in the arm and realized it had been a bullet after all. It was removed and has now joined its place beside the PKM round that struck him in the back. The second bullet was from an AK-47. The bullets flank his Purple Heart, which is framed and mounted in his office.

Gean is a portrait of a fighter. He refuses to give up. He goes fishing and hunting, and has even skied at Winter Park, Colorado, using a mono ski with his knees propped up in front of him and a spring for shock absorption. He has two poles called outriggers that he holds in his hands. He can get on the lifts by himself and ski all day. He wants to ski Vail next and take advantage of the Vail Veterans program. It was started by two WWII veterans of the 10th Mountain Division and allows veterans to ski for free every March. Gean basically does anything he can, and more than most.

"I played the hand I was dealt," says Gean. "I'm not going to sit and mope around."

Gean is 100 percent independent. He is still dating Shannon. He lives by himself and basically does everything he used to do; he just does it in a different way. He now races Baja-style trucks. He has his truck specially fitted with a hand throttle and brakes. He had his first race in Barstow in December 2009. He was doing very well until he blew a tire, and everything attached to the tire ripped in half.

"It was a blast!" said Gean in his interview. He cannot wait for his next race, which is Reno to Vegas in the Spring of 2010. Aside from racing, Gean is going to school to get his teaching certificate and a degree in education. He hopes to teach high school history.

"I am alive today because of Gordon, Bleidorn, and Doc Marchetti," said Gean. "If it weren't for them, Duncan, and those other guys, I would have died on that hill. I'm grateful to them for my life."

Adam Gordon was still in Bagram when he found out Gean and Bleidorn had been moved to Bagram after Asadabad. He took a midnight issue wheelchair and went to talk to Gean. Bleidorn was two beds over from him, so he could talk to him as well. Gean was in the intensive care part of the hospital. Gean was in deep depression trying to come to terms with the fact that he would never walk again. Gordon had his wife call Gean's girlfriend, Shannon, because Gean didn't want to talk to anyone. Gordon convinced his friend to call his girlfriend, and he felt it was beneficial for Gean's mental state.

Gordon was sent to Qatar where he stayed for an entire month. None of the doctors who saw him believed he had a fracture and instead kept reassuring him he had a simple flesh wound. Gordon begged them for an MRI of his foot, but they wouldn't listen and kept telling him to walk on it. Finally, a major accused Gordon of malingering. That was the last straw. Gordon insisted on an MRI, and when they finally did it, they found his heel bone had been split in half.

Gordon's wound needed to heal from the inside out; otherwise a cyst might form. To clean and treat the wound, the nurses inserted a cotton swab at the end of a wooden stick, like a long Q-tip. Only, the nurses were so bad at it that they just gave Gordon the swab, and the perfectionist FO would do it himself. They would give him Demorol, and Gordon would push the swab in to make sure there was a space in the middle.

Shipped to Landstuhl, Germany, then to Walter Reed, he waited to get even basic medication. His wife found a wheelchair, and Gordon sat at a nursing station because the nurse left and never came back, and Gordon was exhausted and in pain from standing on his foot. He returned to Fort Drum and was the acting clear soldier even though he was on crutches. He spent two years trying to get something done because the med board kept switching him to different doctors.

The ortho specialists said his injury was to his foot, so he should see a podiatrist. The podiatrist said it was a bone problem, so they sent him back to ortho. His case manager tried to get him help, but she ended up getting fired because she complained too loudly about the inefficient system. It was a nightmare. Gordon had to get his congresswoman involved. Once she was involved, her office contacted Fort Drum. Then Gordon's paperwork was completed within two weeks, and he was medically retired from the military.

Gordon now lives in Heath, Ohio, with his wife, Melissa. They have one son, Aidan. Gordon currently attends Ohio State University and is getting a degree in history. He is a firefighter for the Heath Fire Department.

Khuong Hang spent the next nine months in the Korangal Valley and saw his unit take hit after hit. Hang's time in the Korangal Valley ended three weeks before Alpha Company rotated home. He was helping build a wooden shelter for a place to live when he slipped and fell off a cliff. His spine was badly damaged. He was MEDEVAC-ed out and flown home to the United States.

Hang returned home, but his wife said the Korangal Valley had changed him. She told Hang she was cheating on him while he was serving in Afghanistan. Hang was glad she didn't tell him until he got home. He might have done something stupid and been killed in combat because of it. Hang is divorced now and lives in Meccina, New York.

Hang's back is permanently damaged. Upon returning home, everything on his body seemed to fall apart. His knees are shot from humping almost three quarters of his body weight up and down the Korangal. His lower back gives him constant problems, and not a day goes by where he is not in pain.

Christopher Quinalty spent two more months in the Korangal before earning a Purple Heart and the right to go home on 2 October 2006. Quinalty had just gotten back from R&R in early October, and the same combat intuition that told the big Texan not to take the low ground at Landigal told him he was going to die in the Korangal. Quinalty said of the deep depression he experience: "I set my affairs in order and made amends for everything I did, or everything I felt I had done. I said my sorry's and my goodbyes to everyone I knew and loved." Then he returned to the Korangal. But he took the mindset that no matter what, he was going to die like a soldier, with honor, no matter what came his way.

When Quinalty came back to the KOP, nothing seemed to have changed. The dusty air was just as heavy as it had been the day he left. Quinalty was sent out in a two-vehicle QRF to help the 3rd Platoon, who had been ambushed. Quinalty's HMMWV later took three RPGs, and he was badly wounded. He regained consciousness to find himself lying on top of their medic, who was KIA.

Quinalty was MEDEVAC-ed to Asadabad where a specialized hand surgeon was able to save his right hand. He spent a month in Bagram and then went to Germany for a month and a half before returning to the United States to begin a long and arduous journey through rehabilitation. On 14 October 2007, a year and a day after he was wounded, SGT Quinalty was medically retired from the military. He and his wife currently reside in New York. He has suffered traumatic brain injury that affects his short-term memory, but his long-term memory is excellent. His right hand has limited feeling and limited use. He and his wife are moving back to Texas.

Neil Yusella watched his platoon take hit after hit. On 17 August, Yusella told Caracciolo to stay behind at the KOP and get some rest. (Caracciolo and Quinalty were his work horses, and they were exhausted.) SPC Joseph Blake took Caracciolo's place in the gun turret. Blake was shot through the head when their convoy was ambushed that day.

Then, on 19 August, Yusella lost his platoon leader when Barclay's convoy was ambushed. Bratland was also wounded, and three other soldiers were KIA.

After Landigal and then the consecutive losses on the seventeenth and nineteenth of August, Yusella had zero faith in

160

his company commander. Yusella said in his interview on 28 March 2010, "I felt he didn't care about any of our lives."

When Yusella went on leave in September, he struggled with what was happening back at the Korangal. He was standing beside his wife at the Sioux Falls airport. He hated the thought of going back to McKnight's command. He said goodbye to his wife and wondered whether he'd see her again. He flew to Texas, but upon landing he stopped. From Texas he was supposed to head back to Afghanistan. Instead he bought a bus ticket back to Sioux Falls.

Yusella was imprisoned for seven months for going AWOL. He was given a bad commendation discharge from the Army. Yusella regrets only one thing: that he let his brother soldiers down. "I feel bad. Talking to Quinalty was kind of hard. He was mad at me. I talked to Crotch. That was kind of hard, too. I haven't talked to Reyna. I talked to Sergeant Gean, too. That was hard. I respect Sergeant Gean. But otherwise I don't regret it."

Yusella was a proven combat veteran, cool under fire and willing to risk his life for his country. But he was determined not to return to a commander he felt did not care about his life or the lives of his soldiers. Instead he chose prison. Yusella now lives in Sioux Falls, South Dakota, with his wife. They are expecting their first child.

[i] It is believed that a Russian Division moved into Asadabad and controlled the Pesch Valley, the Korangal Valley, the Shiriak Valley, and the Waygol Valley. If that is the case, then the Soviets had an entire division (10,000 men) distributed throughout the same area the United States was attempting to control with a single battalion.

[ii] **Jim McKnight:** "This is a good point, and I believe the first time we saw this was in mid-August, but I can't remember. That's when a lot of our one hundred workers or so stopped coming out to the KOP, and we lost a lot of influence with the people. It was the threat of getting murdered!"

[iii] **Jim McKnight:** "Just to make the timeline a little more clear, McQuade stayed at the KOP after Mountain Lion—May first or so to mid-July. Doug Sloan came in for two weeks or so from mid-May to the end of May. Doug and I spent at least three, maybe five, days together before he RIP-ed out, so this Shura would've been with Doug and or Sean still there."

[iv] **Jim McKnight**: "The Shura close to this date would've been with me and Doug Slone because we did one or two together before his headquarters ripped out. Then I brought Sean to at least one to make sure there was good continuity.

"Maybe someone else went to this Shura and had a read that I had said something that ticked someone off to generate this change, but I don't think that was the case. Here is what I remember:

"In mid-May, A company was supposed to be the BN's strike force company and go all over the battle space where the BC needed us. But, one platoon turned out to not be enough in the Korangal, so Lieutenant Colonel Cavoli sent Doug's headquarters there. Somewhere in that time, the enemy had actually gotten on top of O-P-One and placed plunging fire onto the outpost itself. Lieutenant Colonel Cavoli had two comments for me: First was [that] the enemy that we had so severely disrupted during Mountain Lion with a battalion-plus was now regrouping, getting money and weapons back in the valley, and reorganizing for attacks. Second, he was pretty displeased with that the fact that there was plunging fire onto the KOP, so he called me into his office and told me that he was sending me and Tate Preston back to the KOP because we had done such a good job during Mountain Lion in April and May in the Korangal Valley. (Tate captured a lot of enemy weapons and equipment and humped his platoon all over the Korangal and neighboring valleys.) Like Lieutenant Barclay says later on, he and his platoon had been at the relatively safe Khogiyani all this time and missed out on some of this seasoning.

"So, the long point here is, the situation had been digressing since early May—not because of anything anyone did wrong, but because the enemy was regrouping. Attack Company was sent to the Korangal because the enemy was regrouping already; it was not the catalyst to cause it to regroup or gain steam with the population. June third was actually a pretty big firefight, one of the first indicators that the enemy was regrouping, but the Korangalis still loved us at this point; we had about one hundred locals coming to work on our outpost every day. They were renting us their trucks, cooking us food, etc. Later we actually got a report from a source that the June third TIC severely wounded an enemy commander in the area. That was a successful TIC, big time: enemy commander wounded, no friendly casualties!"

[v] Mortar man Sergeant **Bill Wilkinson** was at the KOP when Sean McQuade's platoon was there, and he stayed with Attack Company after McQuade's departure. He had witnessed several of McQuade's Shuras and was watching the Shura in question when A Company first arrived. Stated Wilkinson: "I watch body language. I'm very good at reading people's body language. It was easy to read when several elders stood up and began shouting. That was the first time I'd seen that at a Shura."

Second Platoon, C Company/1/32 Platoon Leader LT **Sean McQuade** said in his interview on 13 February 2010: "I remember thinking, 'Oh shit, this isn't good. This isn't how he should be coming in here and addressing the elders.' It was negative in tone. He was putting them down. His first chat with these guys was all negative—'It's your fault,' 'It's your problem,' instead of, 'Hey, I'm the new commander, let's work together.' The interpreter—the intel guy, THT guy (military intelligence that grow beards)—I remember talking to him, and he said, "This is insane. We've got to stop this." [McKnight] set the tone at the first meeting, and it was negative. He had the chance to come in and start it off right, clean slate.

"[The next day] we [went] down to Landigal to talk to the elders. They were very cold with us. I had never been to Landigal before, but I had talked to the elders and the people there [when we had Shuras] at the KOP and when we made patrols. Never had an issue with them. When we went to Landigal that next day, no one wanted to talk to us. They were all in the fields. They said, 'Hey, we don't want to talk to you, come back later.'

"I said, 'Hey, we were talking last week, what's going on?'

"'No, we don't want to talk.'

"So I didn't push the issue. We started to leave. Back then, we would get water from springs and streams and drink it. And we were out of water, so we stopped and filled up at the local little stream in Landigal, just outside the actual village itself. Filled up our camelbacks, and we started back to the outpost, and it was nine or ten, I think. We got ambushed. It was a perfect ambush spot, and I should have known better, but the way it came down, we were on a foot trail, a goat trail. It winds down. It tends to head back toward the outpost the way the natural terrain, the way the river flows. Is the way you are moving down. We were coming down. And school was out for the grade-school kids. And a couple of them were walking by us. We were in Ranger file, spread out about ten to twenty feet between every soldier. You are always in the low ground the way the terrain is. But there was a rocky knoll to our right, to the north. The river kind of cut through, so it was the perfect point where you were canalized. The enemy, all I remember was I thought it was firecrackers going off. That was the first time I had ever been shot at in anger. 'Holy shit, we're in contact?'

"Guys reacted, NCOs reacted, and we assaulted the position. The problem was [that] we were canalized, so we had to walk down to get out of there. They were only thirty feet from us. We could see them. Guys were running and shooting as we ran down to get around the corner. We dropped some mortars on them, and then we assaulted back through their position. That happened, and then thirty minutes later, the outpost got hit. The re-supply truck was down filling up the water buffalos down at the river. They actually had one or two casualties. That was my truck. They didn't bring any trucks in. They got hit with like four or five RPG rounds. These guys had taken the explosive tips out of the RPG rounds and put in diesel fuel. Later, we got an intel report. When the Marines were there, they had thinly armored vehicles, and the RPGs weren't doing anything to the vehicles. So these guys figured that if they put diesel fuel in it, they'd catch the vehicle on fire and burn the guys alive. No, it didn't work. Not that time luckily.

"That June third we got ambushed, and we were about two thousand meters, sixteen hundred meters, from the outpost, and thirty minutes later the water re-supply truck got hit. Disabled the truck, and then the outpost got hit from two to three sides. So they did another major attack. That kind of opened up my eyes. The tempo increased; the people weren't interacting with us as before. The environment changed in a couple of days.

"My soldiers, they absolutely were like, 'What the hell's going on here, sir? This shit is bad.' Then, as June progressed, the attacks got more bolder. They were pulling off night ambushes. They had some sort of night vision object, which we would find out later. They were using sniper weapons, mortar systems, Dshkas; it just compounded very quickly in a very short period of time. In just a few days Alpha Company had several casualties."
Gary Dales: "I would not dispute the fact that Captain McKnight probably ruffled some feathers. But I don't think that things would have gone much differently in the Korangal. To think the valley would have been tamed or that Captain McKnight caused the whole issue is silly, but it is very possible that Captain McKnight said something to these guys and pissed them off. I know I wanted to go down and arrest all of them myself but we couldn't."

[vi] CPT Brown gets noteworthy praise from many soldiers in the interviews.
Adam Gordon: "Captain Brown was a straight shooter. He was new, so like every new officer he had a lot to learn about commanding an infantry

company, but he trusted his NCOs' counsel. Most commanders don't always do that. Captain Brown was a great leader who kept in touch with his men, asked their opinions, and took it to heart. He was well on his way to being a very good commander. No one wanted him to leave, but battalion didn't ask A Company what we thought."

Chase Gean: "The only good commander we had, great commander, actually, was Captain Brown. That guy would go on patrol with us. He wouldn't say anything; he would just go out with us to observe so he knew what was going on, what we were doing. He wasn't being a chickenshit, staying inside the wire. He would go around and ask the guys general stuff like, 'How are you doing?'—stuff the company commander would do. Captain Brown was out on patrol with us. He was always doing something busy, going out with the squads, doing something to make the company run better."

Josh Lomen: "Captain Jeb Brown was there for such a short period of time, but he brought about a good vibe as opposed to Captain McKnight. People were happy to have Captain Brown."

Shane Wilkinson: "Captain Brown let us NCOs do what NCOs were supposed to do without interfering. We knew what needed to be done, and he didn't interfere with our tactical planning. Captain Brown was a good leader because he relied on his NCOs and let them do their job. For example, when we first got him, we had a mission to a nearby village. Captain Brown wanted us to go to the village on a certain route at a certain time of day. He felt very strongly about that. Me, Sergeant Lomen, my squad leader, and Sergeant Gean sat down and talked with him and told him why we wanted to do something else. He wasn't an officer that put his foot down and said, 'No, do it my way.' He listened and he knew we had experience, and he let us change the route and time of mission, and it turned out fine."

Pat McClure: "Everybody loved Captain Brown. He was fricken awesome. He was a great captain. Captain Brown knew my name, and he was there for such a short period of time. Captain Brown would actually talk to people. He was always out on missions. He was right there. He wanted to lead, instead of stay in his little TOC. That's what it seemed like. A good leader wants to lead by example. He wants to be out there with his men, and he suffered just as much as they did. Captain Brown was one of us."

John Rush: "He was with us for such a short period of time, but while he was with us he did a great job!"

Dan Hewerdine: "He had my respect. Captain Brown had his men's interest at heart and genuinely understood my position and the ANA's. We didn't always agree. My position was mentoring the ANA commander and looking out for the ANA; his was commanding a US Army company, but we had mutual respect and could work together."

165

Nick Bratland: "I wish we would have had him in command over McKnight. He gave a shit about the men under him, and he would actually listen to the guys on the ground. His head wasn't up his ass. He kind of reminds me of Captain Barclay and Sergeant First Class North—all damn good men and great leaders. I have the utmost respect for all of them."

Chris Quinalty: "I preferred Captain Brown's work ethics to Captain McKnight's. He was far more approachable and reasonable when it came to the advice of his NCOs. I wish he would have been there longer."

[vii] 1SG Larry "Big Papa" North gets considerable praise from all the soldiers interviewed. Every single enlisted man interviewed spoke very highly of North. Here are a few. (No one ever called North "Big Papa" to his face, although that was the name by which everyone referred to him. When North read the manuscript, he was surprised to learn he was referred to by the nickname.

Nick Bratland: "Sergeant North is one of those guys that doesn't just speak. He thinks about what he is going to say before he says it. He is very smart and sophisticated, but he is not afraid to get down and dirty. He loves animals. He's tough when he needs to be. He's fair. He will let you know when you are out of line, but after he's done, he will tell you how to fix it so you don't do it again. He is, without a doubt in my mind, the best NCO I ever served under, the best NCO I ever saw in my life. He was one of those guys that would sacrifice his life for his platoon in a heartbeat. I know Sergeant North would have laid down his life for any one of us."

Jae Barclay: "Sergeant North: I couldn't speak more highly of a man. He held that unit together. He trained the guys right."

Adam Gordon: "Sergeant North was a great guy. He was a grizzled old vet. Everybody called him Big Papa. That was his personality. He was a father figure to many of the guys. You didn't want to let him down . . . not because of any consequences but because you'd feel like a piece of shit." You'd feel guilty for failing him. He was the best NCO I ever worked with.

Ben Bleidorn: "Sergeant North was the best platoon sergeant I ever had."

Chris Quinalty: "Sergeant North was a cool-headed individual in every situation but one. That was the day we lost Drawl, Sitton, and Jackson. He was an outstanding NCO and a great leader."

Pat McClure: "Sergeant North is a really smart NCO. He is the best platoon sergeant I've ever had. He kept men's morale up. He is a great leader who knows everything there is to know about the Army. A great man! Great to be around. He is high spirited, always joking around, keeping men happy."

John Rush: "He was great! He really developed Lieutenant Barclay. If there was something he didn't like, he would talk it over with Lieutenant Barclay, and they would address it."

Gary Dales: "Sergeant North was great. He was like a father figure. He was an old country boy. He had a great personality."

Khuong Hang: "Sergeant North told the truth. He told it how it was. If you didn't like it, tough. He wouldn't hold nothing back. He was a great leader."

[viii] LT Barclay received very high praise from all his soldiers.

Benjamin Bleidorn: "Lieutenant Barclay was one of the best officers I've ever served under—bar none. Tactically he was very sound. I think if he had stayed in the Army, he would have made general. He made good decisions quickly. He was not afraid to listen to what Sergeant First Class North had to say. He would take input from his squad leaders and make decisions based on it."

Robert Duncan II: "I loved Lieutenant Barclay. He was a good leader. He listened to everybody. The big thing with lieutenants is if they can listen to a platoon sergeant. He absolutely listened to Sergeant First Class North. That is the whole point of them being there. The leadership of a platoon sergeant helps them, and the lieutenant forms his own leadership."

Josh Lomen: "When Lieutenant Barclay first arrived, I think he did really well for being as green as he was. He was one of the best officers I ever served under. He didn't exclude himself. He didn't say, 'I am the man, and you are not.' He would listen to his squad leaders. He would listen to our platoon sergeant. He would take it all into account and then come up with the best plan based off of all the leadership's knowledge. He would put together what he could, the best that he could, and of course we would go out and do it. Shit rolls downhill—if something came down from higher, he would deflect it."

Pat McClure: "Lieutenant Barclay is a hell of a guy. He is one of the best guys I've ever met. He always led by example. He's not scared of a fight. He's really organized. He sits down, and he talks to his men instead of screaming and yelling at them. He is definitely the best platoon leader I've ever had."

Christopher Quinalty: "He was a great leader and very inspiring. He was one of those approachable guys, he really was. You could come to him and tell him anything—as long as you showed proper respect. He would come and shoot the shit with you if he had a chance. He was brave."

Nick Bratland: "Lieutenant Jae Barclay is the best officer I ever served under." The rest of what Bratland said is included in the text.

John Rush: "Jae Barclay: He was outstanding! He is a great dude! If something was put out that he didn't like, he would address it and let logic prevail. Technically and tactically, he was good to go."

Gary Dales: "Lieutenant Barclay is without a doubt a proven combat leader. The guy wasn't really scared of anything. He always led his troops the way you expected a platoon leader to. He definitely led from the front. He was never afraid to go out of the wire."

167

Khuong Hang: "Lieutenant Barclay was a great leader! He knew us, and he would tell our CO if we weren't mission capable. He looked out for us. Our CO ran us hard. Lieutenant Barclay was a great leader!"

[ix] The crap barrels were where the soldiers relieved themselves. There were no bathrooms at the KOP—not even outhouses. The men would sit on the barrel and defecate. Then, when the foul-smelling, fly-infested barrel was half full, someone would get the duty to burn it. They would pour gasoline in, stir it, and let it burn. When the flames died down, they would pour more gas in, stir it, and let it burn. Soon, the barrel was empty. That was how they took care of human excrement at the KOP. The paradox of the crap barrels was that the user had one of the most magnificent, panoramic views in the world while on it.

[x] In his interview, McKnight said he thought the patrol was too small, but he asked Durgin what he wanted. He said he gave him the number of men he requested.

[xi] McKnight deeply regrets the decision. He said in his second interview on 16 March: "In hindsight, you'd love to have that decision back. In hindsight, yeah, sure as hell, come back in."

[xii] Barclay said in an interview on 29 March 2010: "My concern was not to kill as many bad guys as I could; my concern was to get my guys home alive. I wasn't able to do that. But that was my concern."

[xiii] This incident was verified by Mike Mulherin on 25 March 2010, but Mulherin added this: "Battalion did authorize us to use the main guns on our attached tanks at NTC before we reached the objective—after myself and the attached tank company commander requested their use, instead of having to wait for a number of US casualties, as battalion originally directed—and before we took notional casualties. Before we could execute our hasty plan on the objective, though—I think the objective was called the "Chili Bowl"—we were engaged by the enemy from a nearby ridgeline. We were told to pull off of the objective because battalion was going to call in close air support on the suspected enemy position, but before we could adequately withdraw, battalion dropped notional ordinance with our forces still on the objective. It resulted in further notional casualties. My question in the AAR was why couldn't the commander on the ground control the close air support to avoid the situation where we were not in an appropriate position before the aircraft engaged the enemy position? The response from battalion, which is the correct response, is that the Joint Tactical Air Controller (JTAC) was located in the battalion TOC to allow our close air support to be more flexible for our battalion, and capable to respond to

168

more units—instead of being attached to my company, and being limited on who they could support. The problem with this type of support (Type Three, I think) is it's the most inaccurate type of close air support control. Regardless of whether the battalion thought the commander on the ground had the best idea of what was going on is another issue—and I do remember the BC responding sharply that the battalion TOC had better situational awareness—but my greater concern at the time was our lack of deliberate planning as a battalion and the battalion leadership's desire to move quickly and aggressively with little to no analysis."

[xiv] This series of quotes from Barclay was taken from Bratland's interview. In fact, throughout the book, rarely is a quote from Barclay taken from his interview. Almost always the quote was from someone else's interview. Afterward, the author would approach Barclay and have the quote verified or disproved by him.

[xv] Throughout the writing of this book, in interview after interview, Gordon is praised as being "the best FSO (or FO) in the battalion." This is stated by Barclay, Dales, Gean, Bleidorn, and Duncan. The others all thought very highly of Gordon and his ability at his job.

[xvi] This is from Adam Gordon's interview on 5 February 2010: "I think the worst part of it all was when I got to cover; I could hear Sergeant Gean screaming. He was basically out in the open. I could see him from where I was at. But I had to cross into open ground to get to him. And I had to make the decision: do I go and . . . because he's my buddy. He and I were drinking buddies, and we hung out damn near every day. Making the decision, do I stay here and stay on the radio and try to get these assholes off us, or do I go help Sergeant Gean? That was the hardest decision I have ever had to make. He was just screaming for help. I try not to think about it."

[xvii] Anything "Chosin" meant "battalion." Chosin One-One was the battalion TOC. Chosin Six was his battalion commander.

[xviii] Yusella said this in his interview on 29 March 2010: "Reyna really sucked it up that night. He fought through it. I was impressed with how he kept fighting after he was shot."

[xix] Rush said he thought it was Attack Six but that it could also have been either Attack Five or Attack Four-Five.

[xx] Miguel Salano was not a US citizen. He was serving in the US Army with hopes to become a US citizen. The author was told by Salano's fellow

soldiers that upon return to the United States, after his sixteen-month tour of duty in the Korangal, Salano went to get his citizenship in his uniform. Apparently the line was out the door, and there were a great many people in front of him filing for citizenship. When the officials saw him in uniform, they went out, brought him to the front of the line, and pushed his citizenship through. For once justice was done.

[xxi] Said McKnight in his fifth interview on 25 April 2010: "Praise God that I didn't shoot those guys. I had no idea Hewerdine went out the wire."

[xxii] "I wish things were different," said McKnight in his February and March 2010 interviews. "I wish I had been on that ridge with them that night. But I wasn't."

[xxiii] Said Barclay in his interview on 8 February 2010: "It was a tough conversation. I don't really want to talk about what I said. We went at it."

[xxiv] Probably 95 percent of the quotes given by Barclay were from other soldiers. It was very rare for Barclay to give quotes, although he reviewed the several drafts and admitted when someone else said he spoke. The few times that the author writes Barclay's thoughts occurred because of taped interviews of corrections to rough drafts.

[xxv] **Gary Dales**: "The soldiers didn't like Captain McKnight's leadership style, because, whatever bullshit sandwich the battalion fed us, Captain McKnight made it his orders. He never passed the buck and said, 'Battalion is making us do this.' He said, 'This is what we are going to do; these are my orders.' It was shitty, but Captain McKnight took ownership of the orders. If I was the company commander, I don't think I would have been strong enough to do it. I honestly don't—thinking back about how hard it was. Captain McKnight did it, and they hated him for it."
The author verified with Gary Dales in their interview on 26 March 2010: "In all his interviews, McKnight would not lay any blame on battalion. He said the orders were all his." **Gary Dales** answered affirmatively: "To this day he is still not passing the buck. That is amazing!"

[xxvi] "Yep," said Stevens in his interview on 20 February 2010: "He worked his troops a lot. It was not uncommon. Captain McKnight pretty much worked his company through exhaustion."

[xxvii] Said Dales in his interview on 26 March 2010: "Captain McKnight was honest and trustworthy. The guy didn't have a dishonest bone in his body.

The first thing he did every morning after he woke up was read the Bible. He was just a great guy. He was super smart."

In his interview on 16 March 2010, McKnight said: "A Company 1/32 had the most casualties of any company in the brigade. It's hard to compare, but we had a lot of fighting. As I reflect on that, I am just amazed at the heroism and the rigor and the zeal and the commitment of the soldiers in my company. My company got a lot of accolades because of our successes in Afghanistan. That is not because of anything I did or my bosses did; it is because of guys like Jae Barclay and Chase Gean, who did extremely brave things. The list of guys is long, and so is the list of valor awards and Purple Hearts for guys who gave everything to defeat the enemy. I let some of them down with the decisions I made, and I feel bad about that. But I tried my hardest and did what I thought was best. But I also feel very proud of what we did accomplish."

About the Author

James F. Christ has a fascination for military history. He has traveled extensively throughout Europe, Africa, and parts of Asia visiting battle sites such as Normandy, Zululand, Pearl Harbor, and Jerusalem.

Christ is currently working on additional books about the Afghanistan War. He lives in Chandler, Arizona, with his two beloved sons, Nolan and Trace.

For further reading by Christ:

IWO; ASSAULT ON HELL; 2012
MISSION RAISE HELL, Naval Institute Press; 2006
BATTALION OF THE DAMNED, Naval Institute Press; 2007
MEMORIES FROM TUSKEGEE, Battlefield Publishing; 2008
THE BONE YARD, Battlefield Publishing; 2008
MORGHAB CANYON, Battlefield Publishing; 2008
KAMDESH, Battlefield Publishing; 2008
SHUDERGAY, Battlefield Publishing; 2011
TSANGAR, Battlefield Publishing; 2012
YAKAH CHINAH, Battlefield Publishing; 2012
HELL IS THE KORENGAL, Battlefield Publishing; 2012

Made in United States
Orlando, FL
25 April 2024

46180033R00104